I0491025

ART BOOKS

FROM CRESCENT MOON PUBLISHING

Leonardo da Vinci
by James Pearson

Early Netherlandish Painting
by Rosalind Mutter

Piero della Francesca
by Naomi Haskell

Giovanni Bellini
by Julia Davis

Eric Gill: Nuptials of God
by Anthony Hoyland

Minimal Art and Artists In the 1960s and After
by Laura Garrard

Postwar Art
by George Knighton

Vincent van Gogh: Visionary Landscapes
by Stuart Morris

Max Beckmann
by Stuart Morris

Egon Schiele: Sex and Death in Purple Stockings
by D. Simon Eade

Mark Rothko: The Art of Transcendence
by Julia Davis

Jasper Johns
by L.M. Poole

Brice Marden
by Laura Garrard

Frank Stella: American Abstract Artist
by James Pearson

COROT

COROT

BY SIDNEY ALLNUTT

CRESCENT MOON

First published 1918. This edition © 2020.

Set in Book Antiqua 10 on 14pt.
Designed by Radiance Graphics.

Thanks to the authors and publishers quoted.

British Library Cataloguing in Publication data

ISBN-13 9781861716170 (Pbk)
ISBN-13 9781861717733 (Pbk)
ISBN-13 9781861717269 (Hbk)

CRESCENT MOON PUBLISHING
P.O. Box 1312, Maidstone, Kent, ME14 5XU
Great Britain, www.crmoon.com

CONTENTS

NOTE ON THE TEXT

The text is from *Corot* by Sidney Allnutt, published by T.C. &
E.C. Jack, London and Frederick A. Stokes, New York, 1918 as
part of the Masterpieces In Colour series, edited by T. Leman
Hare.

The illustrations discussed in the book are included in the
illustrations section, along with many other works.

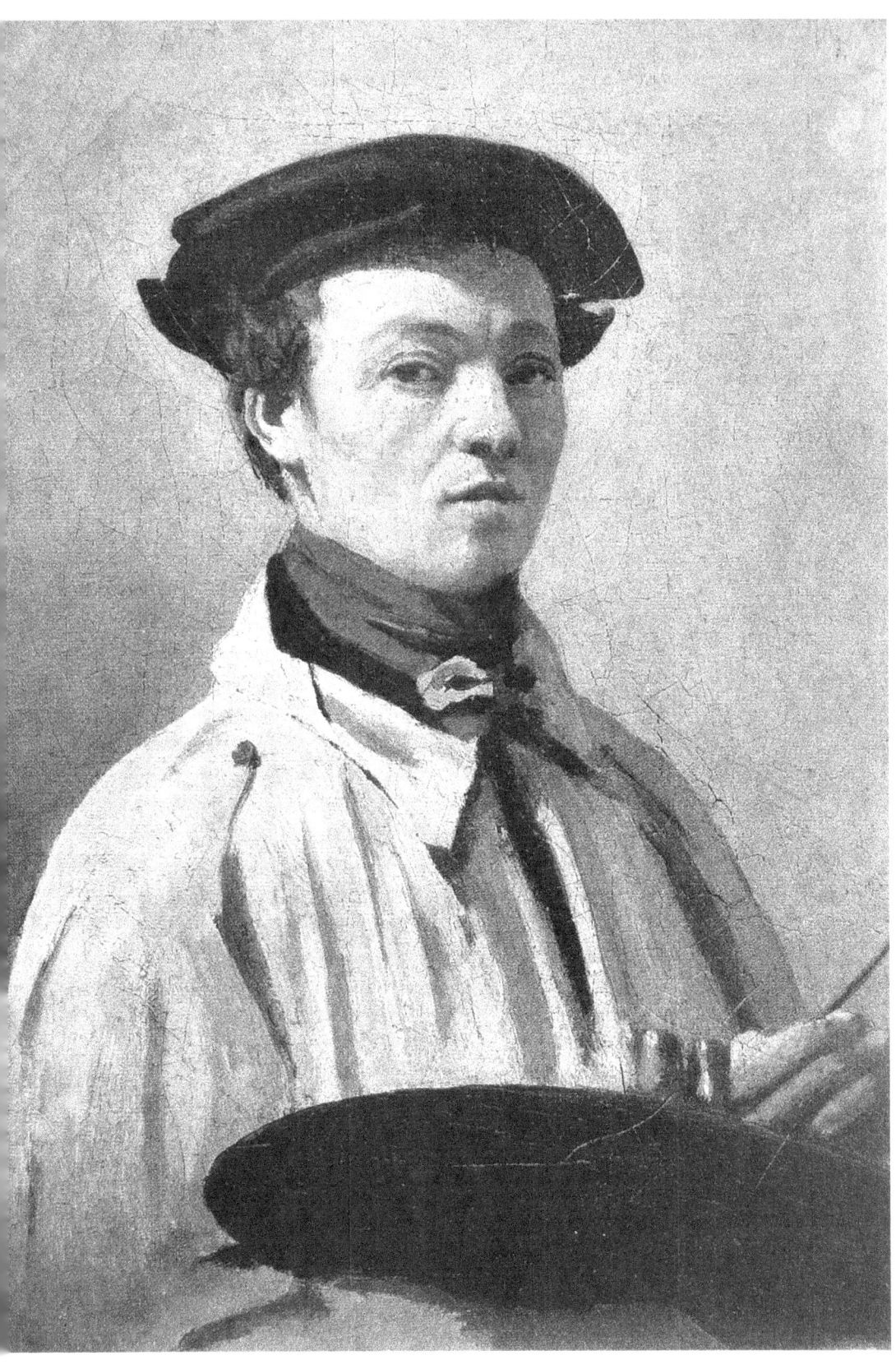

J.B.C. Corot, Self-Portrait, 1835, Uffizi Gallery

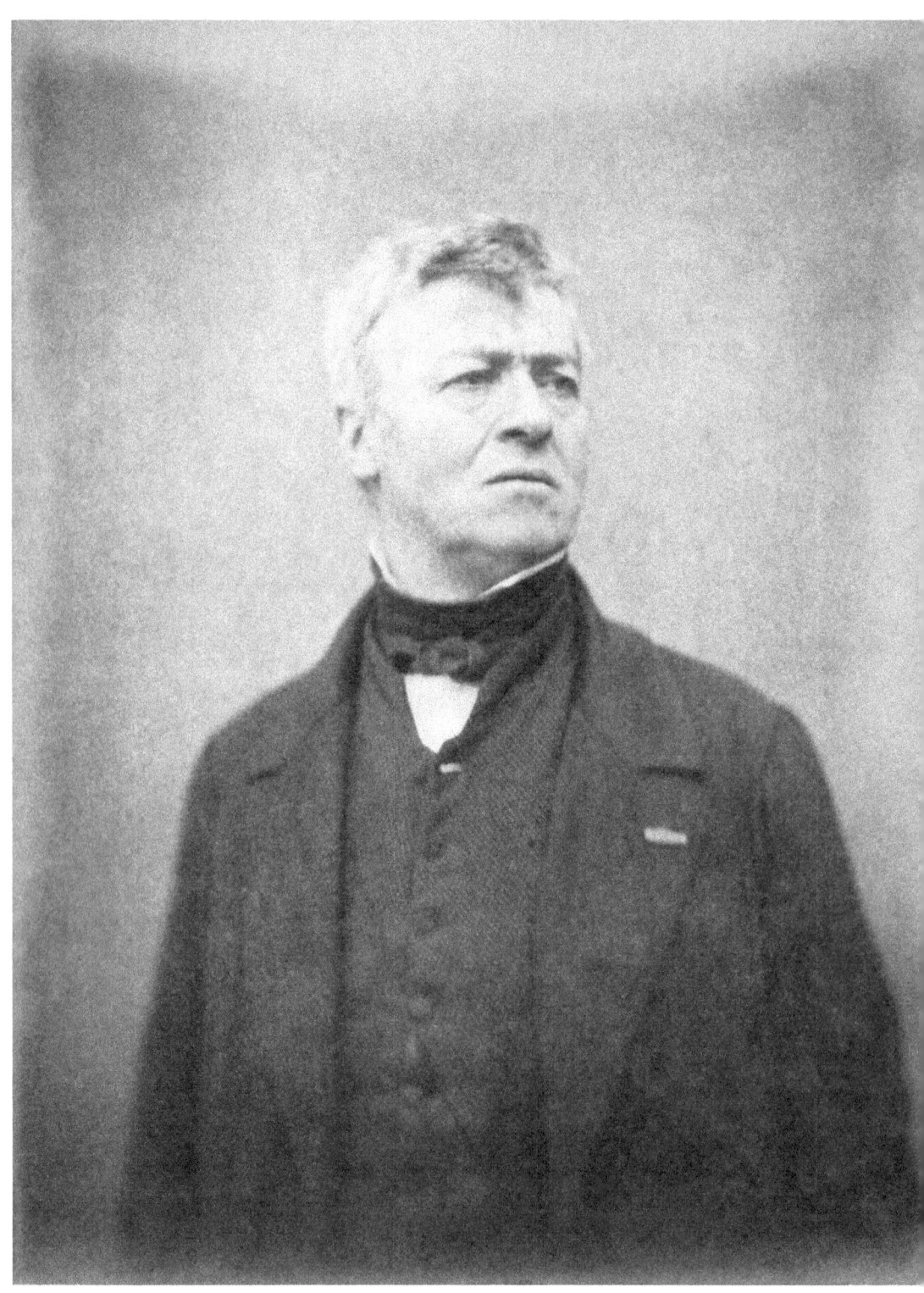

J.B.C. Corot, c. 1850, by Victor Laisné (Lainé)

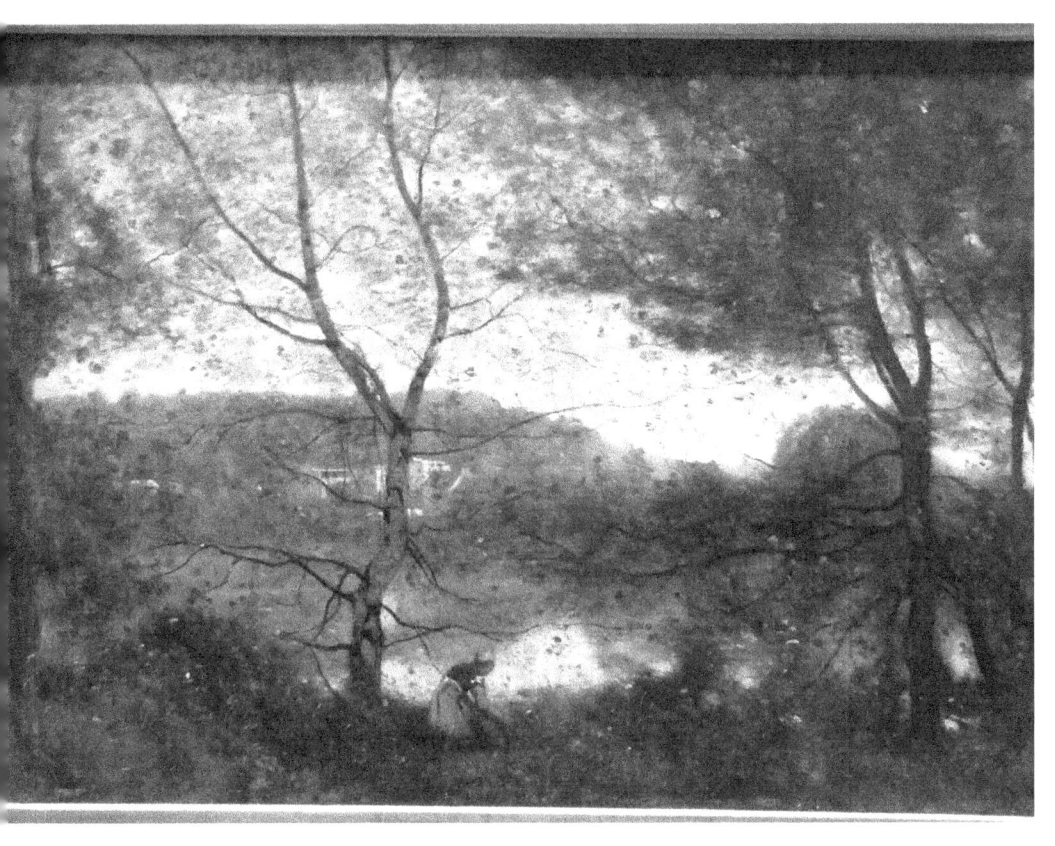

J.B.C. Corot, Ville d'Avray, 1870, Getty Museum, Los Angeles

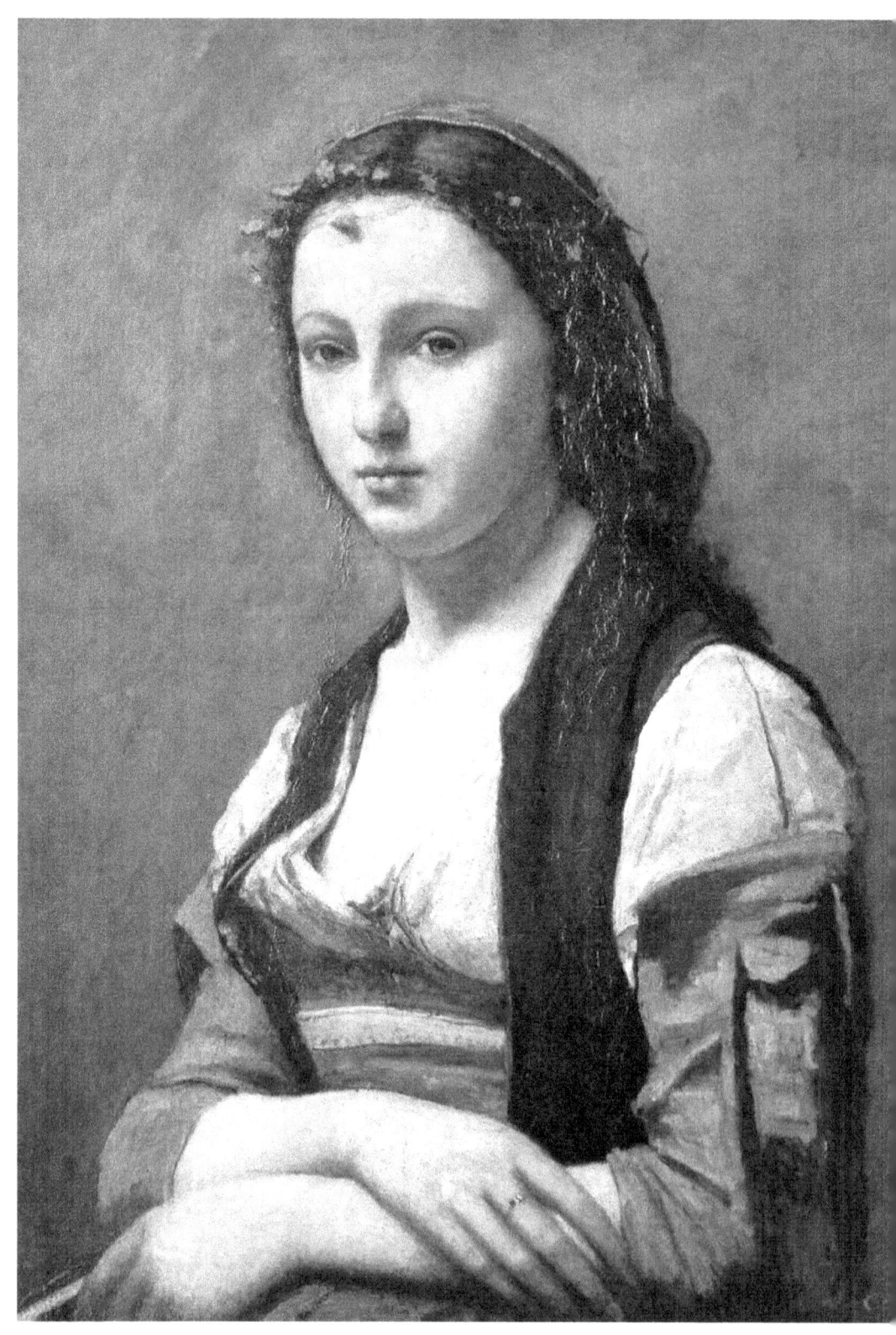

J.B.C. Corot, Woman With a Pearl, 1868-70, Louvre, Paris

The work of Jean Baptiste Camille Corot has been steadily rising in the estimation of the instructed ever since he won his first notable successes in 1840. During the greater part of the artist's life-time the rise was very gradual, and he would have been astonished indeed if he could have known how rapid it was to be after his death. It is by no means only a rise in the selling prices of such of his works as come into the market – a Corot has something more than a collector's value; but figures are in their way eloquent, and when we find a work ("Le Lac de Garde") for which the painter was glad to get 800 francs selling for 231,000 francs within thirty years of his death, the rapid growth in the fame of the painter is materially evidenced.

There are fashions in art as in everything else: for reasons which the dealers could often disclose if they would, this or that artist's work is suddenly boomed, and for a time commands absurdly big prices in the auction rooms, only to find its proper level again when it is no longer to anybody's interest to maintain an artificial valuation. But it is difficult to believe that the passing of years will do anything to diminish the fame of Corot, or lessen the prices which connoisseurs are willing to pay for the possession of his work. Rather will both increase, there is reason to think, as under the winnowing of Time's wings the chaff is separated from the grain, and many a painter hailed as a master to-day is scorned if not forgotten. For whatever may happen, it is impossible to believe that the work of Corot will ever become old-fashioned. There is in it something that does not belong to one time, but to all times; not to one place, but to all places. It is elemental and universal, and instinct with a vitality and youth that unnumbered to-morrows can have no power to destroy.

Even those critics who most strongly opposed the canons Corot professed – and there were many of them – were often unable to condemn a heresy in which faith was so justified by works: coming to curse, like Balaam, they remained to bless. A far more trying ordeal the artist had to undergo in the intemperate rhapsodies of enthusiastic admirers. But neither censure or praise, the scepticism of his own people, or the indifference of the picture-buying public, could tempt him to deviate from the path that for him was the right one. "Vive la conscience, vive la simplicité!" he used to say. His creed was in the words, and he lived up to it.

He claimed for the artist an entire independence. "You must interpret nature with entire simplicity, and according to your personal sentiment, altogether detaching yourself from what you know of the old masters or of contemporaries. Only in this way will you do work of real feeling. I know gifted people who will not avail themselves of their power. Such people seem to me like a billiard-player, whose adversary is constantly giving him good openings, but who makes no use of them. I think that if I were playing with that man, I would say, 'Very well, then, I will give you no more.' If I were to sit in judgment, I would punish the miserable creatures who squander their natural gifts, and I would turn their hearts to cork." Again he says – "Follow your convictions. It is better not to exist than to be the echo of other painters. As the wise man says, if one follows, one is behind." And again – "Art should be an individual expression of the verities, an ardour that concedes nothing."

It is on the face of it rather a hopeless task to attempt to trace the artistic pedigree of a painter who, at all costs, will be individual with "an ardour that concedes nothing"; and it would not help much towards an understanding of him. At the same time, it would be a mistake to suppose that Corot was quite so independent of the influences around as, perhaps, he imagined himself to be. "Artists," says Shelley in a notable utterance, "cannot escape from subjection to a common influence which arises out of an infinite combination of circumstances belonging to the times in which they live, though each is in a degree the author of the very influence by which his being is thus pervaded."

Thus Corot took his part in the revolt against classicism in France, with which the name of the little village of Barbizon is so inseparably associated. He coloured it, and was coloured by it – so much was inevitable; but his intense individuality none the less preserved him in an aloofness from what I may be permitted to call the broad path of the movement. And as he grew older, so far from becoming more affected by his contemporaries, he only seemed more and more to discover himself.

Before all things Corot was an idealist – a painter of ideas rather than of actualities; which, of course, does not in any way discount his simple sincerity. His landscapes give the idea of a place or an effect rather than its exterior appearance. The rendering of a beautiful passage of colour, of a gracious form, or a delicate play of light and shade, was never held to be sufficient. Within the body of phenomena he saw the throbbing heart and luminous soul of Nature revealed; and it was the very heart and soul of his subject that he strove to prison in his pigments. At the same time, dreamer as he was, there was always in him a healthiness and sanity rare indeed amongst those who are given to seeing visions.

I remember a studio gathering at which Corot was discussed. I wish the master, who always loved to be praised by those who could understand and were sincere, could have heard what was said of him. At length some one said, "Corot was a great artist. It is true that he also happened to be a great painter." The words seemed to me to have meanings.

A painter is a man who does something; an artist one who is something. The statement may not be new, but it is true; and what it involves is, I think, too often forgotten.

In considering what a painter has done it is natural enough to be preoccupied with his method, to become immersed in an analysis of his technique. There will be an attempt to determine whether he is faithfully obedient to the accepted canons, or modifying and adapting, if not it may be defying them. In the latter case an endeavour must be made to find a solution for the question whether these progressive or revolutionary activities are justified in their result.

It is criticism of this sort that fills innumerable studios with a jargon unintelligible to all but those who are, so to say, "in the trade" in one way or another, and can speak with a craftsman knowledge – of technical terms if of nothing else. Such talk is often futile enough, a breaking of butterfly nothings upon a ponderous wheel of words; though it can, on occasion, be useful enough. In any case only a few, comparatively speaking, are likely to be either interested or benefited.

It is altogether another matter when an artist is approached. How he conveys his message is of much less importance than what is conveyed. He may be poet, painter, or musician, but the need for understanding what he does is infinitely less than that of learning what he is. This is not to say that, in the case of the artist, technique is beneath consideration; but it is to say that it must not be considered first. Trembling script sometimes give the authentic gospel its birth in words, and a true vision may be recorded by an uncertain hand. To lose sight of the artist in contemplating the technique of the work by which he reveals himself is to sacrifice the substance for the shadow.

Corot was a great artist. To him his art was not a trade or an amusement, still less a trick, but a religion. He worshipped with an unceasing diligence and intensity before the chosen altar of his adoration. Less than his best he dared not offer there. Nothing that was not wholly honest and true could be acceptable. What a magnificent character he gives to himself, all unconsciously, in confessing to M. Chardin an artistic sin! "One day I allowed myself to do something chic; I did some ornamental thing, letting my brush wander at will. When it was done I was seized with remorse; I could not close my eyes all night. As soon as it was day, I ran to my canvas, and furiously scratched out all the work of the previous evening. As my flourishes disappeared, I felt my conscience grow calmer, and once the sacrifice was accomplished I breathed freely, for I felt myself rehabilitated in my own sight."

What would some of our painters say to a conscience so tyrannous?

It is, for me, impossible to look at Corot's work without feeling that his was, if I may put it so, a monastic nature. Here is a serene and cloistered art, something secluded from the traffic of the everyday world, a vision intense rather than wide. I think of Corot as a priest at the altar of one of Nature's innermost sanctuaries celebrating sacramental mysteries. Every picture that came from him is an elevation of the Host.

This is the quality in his work, much more than a fastidious refinement nearer the surface, that gives it so high a distinction. Hung in a gallery among other pictures, a Corot does not clamour for notice. It is much too quiet in matter and manner for that; but, after awhile, it draws the eye, and when it has done so its hold is secure. The surrounding canvases almost invariably begin to look a little vulgar in its neighbourhood. And this not only because rioting colour might well look blatant by the side of the tender greys and greens and rose flushes that the artist loved so well, but because the spirituality of which those tones are merely the expression places the Corot upon another and a higher plane.

To come upon a Corot in a gallery is like stepping out of the noisy glare of the market-place into the cool stillness of a church. Market-places are good things, and the noisy crowd is perhaps only noisy because it is doing its appointed work in a right hearty fashion; but the Presence seems nearer in the silence of the church. The silence is not dead, but quick with soundless speech. So with a Corot picture; its quietness is the very antipodes of stagnation. It seems to spread far beyond the limits of the frame in ever-widening waves, until everything around is subdued.

The only other works of art which have ever given me quite the same impression in this direction are one or two of those dreaming Buddhas that, wherever they may be, seem to be shrined in a stillness emanating from themselves.

From first to last Corot was as independent as he was industrious. He strove always to see Nature with his own eyes, and to keep his vision clear and simple. Whether or not other painters had a grander or nobler vision was nothing to him. It mattered only that he should be true to the grace that was his own. "I pray God every day," he said, "that He will keep me a child; that is to say, that He will enable me to see and draw with the eye of a child." That prayer was surely answered, for never did an artist look out upon the world with a more direct simplicity, or with eyes more delicately sensitive to the appeal of beauty.

It was seldom the obviously picturesque that appealed to him. He seemed instantly to apprehend the most elusive of the beauties in the scene before him. That death-bed utterance of Daubigny is significant: "Adieu; I go above to see if friend Corot has found me new landscapes to paint." That was it: Corot never failed to find new landscapes to paint, for his eye was keen enough to pierce through what seemed commonplace, and discover the underlying beauty. Starting off on one of his innumerable sketching excursions, he remarks to a friend that he has heard bad accounts from painters of the country for which he is bound, but adds that he has no doubt he will find pictures there. And, of course, he found them. The pictures are always there, though the faculty of seeing them is rare.

No one ever worked more constantly and faithfully from Nature, or became more intimately acquainted with the subtle outward expressions of her innermost moods; but the profound knowledge thus gained was only treated as the poet treats a wide vocabulary; as a means of expression, not as in itself worth exploitation. The scene before him was not recorded as a collection of facts, but as it had stirred his emotions, and as it was, in a sense, transformed by his vivid imagination. The resulting picture is the record of an adventure of the soul; the outward reality is not lost, but rather realised in a strange intensity. "See," said Corot, pointing to one of his landscapes, "see the shepherdess leaning against the trunk of that tree. See, she turns suddenly. She hears a field-mouse stirring in the grass."

Of how the artist went to work when he had "found" a new landscape some notion may be gained from M. Silvestre's description. "If Corot sees two clouds that at first sight appear to be equally dark, he will, before building up the whole harmony of his picture on one or other of them, apply himself to discover the difference he knows must exist. Then, when he has decided on the darkest as well as the lightest tone in the scene before him, the intermediate values readily take their places, and subdivide themselves indefinitely before his discerning eyes. These values, from the most positive to the most vague, call to one another and give answer, like echo and voice. When the artist sees he can divide the principal values of the landscape before him into four, he does so by numbering the different parts of his rough sketch from 1 to 4, 4 standing for the darkest and 1 for the lightest patch, while the intermediate tones are represented by 2 and 3. This method enables Corot, with the help of any old pencil and any scrap of paper, to make records of the most transitory effects seen upon a journey. Corot was not a man to make an inventory of his sentiments, and the fact that he made such records proves that they were sufficient for his own purposes. As a rule he first of all puts in his sky, then the more important masses in the middle of the composition, then those to the left and to the right; he then picks out the forms of the reflections in the water, if there is water, and so establishes the planes of his picture, his masses falling in one behind the other while one watches him. Sometimes he proceeds in a less orderly way; for it goes without saying that his methods are the methods of freedom, and not the invariable recipes of a pedant. He runs an unquiet eye over every part of the canvas before putting a touch in place, sure that it does no violence to the general effect. If he makes haste he may become clumsy and rough, leaving here and there inequalities of impasto. These he afterwards removes with a razor, as if he were shaving his landscape, and leaving himself free to profit by such accidents of surface as are happy in effect."

The picture of Corot sketching in shorthand shows him when the long and close study of Nature had enabled him to generalise with confidence, and when a memory, always retentive, had been trained to a pitch that made it far more reliable than any sketchbook memoranda. Although he always expressed impatience with the idea that anything worth doing could be done merely by taking pains, Corot was the least apt of men to spare any pains that were essential to his purpose; and nothing could be farther from the truth than the suggestion sometimes made, that he was wanting in this respect. To generalise as he generalised is not to be careless of detail, but the very reverse: it implies a knowledge so complete of every element in a landscape that those belonging to a particular view of it can be selected with an unerring judgment, and what is non-essential eliminated. "Put in as much as you like at first, and afterwards efface the superfluity," is a bit of advice that comes from Corot himself. It was not a strikingly original remark, but it could not have been made by other than a conscientious worker.

It is certainly a mistake to suppose that Corot was careless of details in the sense that he did not give them due consideration; but he always realised that details were details after all. "I never hurry to the details of a picture," he said; "its masses and general character interest me before anything else. When those are well established, I search out the subtleties of form and colour. Incessantly and without system I return to any and every part of my canvas."

There is a note in Mr. George Moore's *Modern Painting* that seems to throw some illumination upon Corot's manner of looking at his subject. Mr. Moore came upon the artist, an old man then, "in front of his easel in a pleasant glade. After admiring his work, I ventured to say: 'What you are doing is lovely, but I cannot find your composition in the landscape before us.' He said, 'My foreground is a long way ahead.' And sure enough, nearly two hundred yards away, his picture rose out of the dimness of the dell, stretching a little beyond the vista into the meadow."

I think Corot's foreground had a habit of being a considerable way ahead.

To most, Corot is "the man of greys," the painter of the twilight. Without for a moment suggesting that this is true in so far as it seems to hint that his art had very narrow limitations, I am certainly inclined to believe that the general eye has fixed itself upon his most characteristic and most valuable work. The two dawns, as the old Egyptians called them, Isis and Nephthys, the dawn of day and the dawn of night, revealed themselves to Corot with a fulness to be measured only perhaps in part by the manner in which he has revealed them to us. The stillness, the freshness, the indescribable tremor of awakening life, the curious sense of a remoteness in familiar things, the expectancy as of some momentous revelation, all that goes to make the mystery and magic of the dawn, he knew how to translate into subtle yet easily understandable terms of form, and tone, and colour. It was a miracle to which he seemed to have found the key – perhaps by means of that prayer to be "kept a child." Over and over again he invoked the dawn to appear upon his canvas, and never in vain. In ever-varying robes of loveliness, but the same in all of them, the dawn responded to his call.

Grey dawn! The words had a cold and gloomy sound until Corot interpreted them, taking the gloom away and leaving of the cold only the delicious shiver of the morning freshness. Beautiful almost as the dawn itself – born of it as they were – are those wonderful pearly greys of his. His palette seemed to hold an infinite range of them, each pure and perfect in itself, and each in a true harmonic relation to the others.

And if the painted dawns are beautiful, they are also true; they carry instant conviction of their absolute verity. There is only one thing that can make a painted canvas do this, and that is truth of tone, and of tone-values Corot made himself a master, mainly because he never ceased to be a student. He retained the eye of a child, but his mind became stored with the accumulated experience of many long hours that were only not laborious because the work was a delight. And great as the store grew in process of time, he was adding to it up to the last.

Here is a picture by Albert Wolff of the artist at the age of 79, when the hand of Death was already stretched out towards him. "An old man, come to the completion of a long life, clothed in a blouse, sheltered under a parasol, his white hair aureoled in reflections, attentive as a scholar, trying to surprise some secret of nature that had escaped him for seventy years, smiling at the chatter of the birds, and every now and again throwing them the bar of a song, as happy to live and enjoy the poetry of the fields as he had been at twenty. Old as he was, this great artist still hoped to be learning."

It is altogether an important thing about Corot that he was always singing – in season and out of season I was about to say, when I remembered that he would probably have declared that it was always singing-time. He went to his work carolling like a lark, though with a somewhat robuster organ, and snatches of song punctuated his brush strokes. The day's work done, he broke out into melody in earnest, and sang to himself, to his friends, at home or abroad, with equal vigour and enjoyment. We are told that on one occasion his irrepressible song broke out at an official reception, doubtless to the confusion of dignities and the shocking of many most respectable people.

I cannot but think that something of music found its way into Corot's pictures. They look as if they could have been done in music as well as they were done in paint. In a way they were: if there was always a song on his lips, surely there was also a song at his heart. One may say that his paintings were built to music like the walls of Thebes. They are haunted by sweet harmonies, and seem charged with hidden melodies that tremble on the verge of sound.

Many of those who read may shake their heads at this attempt to make a confusion of two arts, but my apology shall take the form of a quotation from Corot himself. Moved to sudden emotion by a magnificent view, he exclaimed, "What harmony! What grandeur! It is like Gluck!" I think the man who said that may possibly have painted a little music, without caring for a moment whether he was confusing the arts or not. Perhaps he felt that painting and music were more nearly related than a certain school of critics can allow itself to admit. But that is by the way.

When in Paris he was frequent in his attendances at concerts and the opera, and indeed music always drew him with a power only second to that of his chosen mistress – painting. As the twig is bent the tree will grow – it may be that had the accidents of his early environment been other than they were, his name would be famous as that of a great composer instead of a great painter. Fortunately we do not know what we may have missed, while we are fully conscious of what we have gained.

•

The father of Corot the painter was Louis Jacques Corot, who, if he escaped being altogether a hairdresser, only did so by a narrow margin. One would rather like to imagine him as another "Carrousel, the barber of Meridian Street."

> "Such was his art, he could with ease
> Curl wit into the dullest face;
> Or to a goddess of old Greece
> Lend a new wonder and a grace.
> The curling irons in his hand
> Almost grew quick enough to speak;
> The razor was a magic wand
> That understood the softest cheek."

Such was Carrousel, according to Aubrey Beardsley's ballad, and such Louis Jacques Corot should surely have been, if only to make his son more easily explainable; but, as a matter of fact, he appears at an early age to have forsaken the high art of hairdressing for more strictly commercial pursuits. He became a clerk, and his wife's assistant manager.

For Madame Corot was a business woman – very much so. She was a native of Switzerland, and evidently of the practical nature that so often distinguishes the Swiss people. A woman of property in a moderate way, and two years older than her husband, as well as a capable manager, she does not appear by any means to have allowed marriage to submerge her own personality. As a *marchande de modes* she was a distinct success. Fashion found its way to her establishment in the Rue du Bac, and the name Corot became a hall-mark of elegance.

Perhaps her son owed more to his mother than has sometimes been suspected. Corot himself remarked that a skill equal to that of the painter was often shown by the costumier in the blending of colours – indeed he went farther, and said as much of a certain flower-seller of his acquaintance and her bouquet-making. Really, when one comes to think of it, he may be said to come of artists on both sides, for if his father was scarcely as much of a hairdresser as we should like him to be, his paternal grandfather's claim to the description is beyond criticism.

Under these circumstances it is a little sad that, when he had completed his educational career without winning any considerable distinction, it was decided to make a draper of him. There is every evidence that, in so far as the attempt went, he made a very bad draper indeed. I do not know how long it took him to come to the conclusion that he would never make a good one – not very long, I should say – but after a trial of six years or so, it would seem that his father had arrived at the same conclusion. When his son declared his intention of abandoning drapery and of becoming a painter, Corot *père* did not offer any strenuous objection. He thought that the young man was a fool, and said so, with possibly a little bitterness, but on the whole with resignation. What was more to the point, he made a small provision, so that his son might live while "amusing himself."

The provision in question was certainly a small one – 1500 francs a year – but it prevented Corot from ever knowing the extremities of poverty to which some of his brilliant contemporaries were reduced. As he said, he could always count on "shoes and soup" – and shoes and soup, if not much in themselves, can often bridge the gulf that lies between hope, or even content, and despair. Moreover, Corot's wants were few. Throughout his life he had the simplest tastes, and his only extravagance was a charity that gave without measure and never thought about return.

However, figure to yourself Corot fully embarked on his career as a painter. He is, roughly, twenty-five years of age, and for stock-in-trade has glowing health, a certain familiarity with pencil and brush already acquired, an unquenchable enthusiasm, and so many francs a year. On the whole it is the outfit of a very happy and fortunate young man.

Once emancipated from the compulsions of drapery he lost no time in setting to work. He went straight to Nature, and even at this time produced work that bore a hall-mark as distinctive as that of his later years. He worked also in the studios of Michallon and of Bertin, and if they did him no good (and there is little reason to suppose such a thing), they at least did him no harm. Already he was too keenly engaged upon a line of his own.

Around Ville d'Avray, where his father had bought a house, he found numberless subjects ready to his hand, subjects of which nothing that he saw in his wide wanderings could ever make him tired. He also had an experience in Morvan. I shall venture to quote from Mr. Everard Meynell's "Corot and his Friends," concerning it.

> "He went, presently, to the little hamlet of Morvan, whose blacksmith gave him hospitality. As a member of a farrier's numerous family, with the forge for sitting-room, and its fires to assuage the cold of mortals and of metals, and soup for fuel, and the blue smock of the country for raiment, Corot saved money. He saved money out of the 1200 francs of his allowance; even the cost of canvas and paints did not bring his expenditure to three francs a day. His austerity meant Rome, but it was not a hard road for him to follow. Never was a man less provoked to any of the pampered ways of living."
> "It was in Morvan that Corot picked up with the peasant, and found

in him many things fit to be learned. He learnt about soups, and pipes, and blouses, and the habit of the sunrise; and nothing that he learned did he forget. Soups, and pipes, and blouses, and the sunrise lasted him till the end of his life. These things, like the honest humour and good-comradeship of a man afield, were in his blood; but Morvan and Morvan's blacksmith, and daily things done with the Morvan peasantry, developed the peasant in the painter. Corot's was nearer to the peasant's character than Millet's even; for the emotional gloom of Millet's outlook, his sense of the price paid for life, his sense of death and toil, of the significance of the seed and the scythe, made him a person too great and dreadful to be familiar with those for whom he thought and felt. Corot's laugh and song, his raillery and content, were things to be friends with."

I think that in the foregoing passage the influence upon Corot of the Morvan visit, though it may well have been a memorable one, has been perhaps a trifle exaggerated. Surely he must have "picked up" with the peasant long before, and found out how much he had in common with the dweller on the soil. And will the comparison with Millet fully bear examination? I doubt it. The extraordinary delicacy and refinement of Corot's vision is at least a thing as foreign to the peasant as the tense emotionalism of Millet; and I suspect that the deep-rooted content of the one was as much removed as the implicit revolt of the other from the people with whom in their several ways they were both so much in sympathy. That in personal relations Corot got nearer than Millet to his peasant friends is more than probable. If not more understandable in reality, he seemed so in daily intercourse with those as simple and direct as himself. There was nothing in him to repel. His gay and expansive nature invited a confidence that was seldom withheld, except by those too distrustful and secretive themselves to understand it.

The first visit to Italy, undertaken in 1825, marks an epoch in the life of Corot, as in that of many another painter. But though it widened his outlook, and taught him much that otherwise he might never have learned, it did not tempt him to any deviation from the simple principles that all through his life guided him in the practice of his art. All the inducements which Italy could offer were not sufficient to make him incline to use other eyes than his own when painting. He seems to have treated the Masters in an unusually cavalier manner. Nature in Italy interested him much more than Art in Italy: he was more concerned with sunsets than with Michelangelo.

As was his custom, Corot was always at work in Italy, "sitting down" with his usual happy knack in finding the right spot, and painting what he saw as he saw it, with careful fidelity to his own beautiful way of looking at things. Sometimes he worked from models in his room, but whether indoors or out, day after day found him painting, painting with unabated enthusiasm and ever-fresh delight.

And he made friends, as always – among them d'Aligny, who was the first to take the true measure of the then somewhat awkward young man. "D'Aligny," says Mr. Everard Meynell, "was the discoverer of his genius and its advertiser; for having found Corot at work on the 'Vue du Colisée,' now hanging in the Louvre, he made a formal statement of his admiration at 'Il Lepre' (a café in Rome much frequented by painters) that night. 'Corot, who sings songs to you, and to whom you listen or call out your ribald chaff,' said he, 'might be master of you all!'"

The friendship lasted until the death of d'Aligny in 1874, and Corot never forgot the generous praise that had so encouraged him during those early days in Rome.

In 1827 Corot exhibited for the first time in the Salon. The two pictures which bore his name were not unnoticed, but no one was sufficiently interested to purchase them. It was indeed fortunate on the whole that he was assured of "shoes and soup" from other sources than his art, for it was not until 1840 that it brought him any monetary reward worth mentioning. But it would be beside the mark to say that he had to endure any remarkable period of neglect. It must be remembered that his career as a painter did not seriously begin until he was of an age when many artists have already secured something of a position for themselves. His work, too, was not of such a description as to make any sensational impact upon the attention of the art-loving public.

Before he returned from his first visit to Rome he had, however, made his mark in some measure, had been hailed by a few discerning critics as one of the elect. The enthusiastic testimony of d'Aligny and one or two others had been endorsed with signatures that carried some weight – only at home was he still held to be an amateur. His right to a place among the more notable artists of his time was no more questioned, except by those whom ignorance or prejudice had rendered incapable of sane judgment.

Once more, and again, he visited Italy, painting as he went, and what was much more to the purpose, filling with magic pictures the tablets of his mind: but I doubt if these subsequent visits carried him far beyond the point he had arrived at during the first. Each day he was gaining more knowledge and greater dexterity, but his point of view was never seriously modified. Italy gave to his delicacy some of its strength, invested the most tender-hearted of painters with the touch of sternness that could alone save his work from becoming invertebrate: but it could not materially alter his habit of vision, or turn into dramatic shape an inherently lyrical gift. He saw Nature as a song in France first of all and last of all; Italy only helped him to give the song a more severe metrical basis than it might otherwise have possessed. Much that was sweet in Corot it would seem that the relentless landscapes and pitiless skies of Italy helped to make strong.

From 1840 onwards one may say that Corot was steadily growing into fame. In that year two of his pictures were bought by public authorities, and thus, for the first time, an official imprimatur was set upon his increasing reputation. He never knew the feverish delight of awaking one morning to find himself famous. The value of his work was only very slowly recognised, and as his paintings attracted more and more notice a heavy fire of hostile criticism was opened upon them: with no more effect than to make him smile as he went upon his way.

Some of these egregious criticisms are so utterly beside the mark that it is difficult to believe them anything but the result of a wilful misapprehension on the part of the critics. They seem to be inspired by venom and spite when read to-day: but in their own time they probably fairly represented the serious opinions of many who thought they were defending legitimate art against a spreading anarchy. It is even possible that such as Nieuwerkerke, who, as Mr. Meynell records, was "overheard describing Corot as a miserable creature who smeared canvases with a sponge dipped in mud," honestly believed that he was administering a well-deserved castigation to a charlatan. It is more than likely that many of us are making mistakes almost as serious to-day, so we need not find such an attitude incredible.

There were other critics at this same period who were less hampered by preconceived notions, and came to a very different conclusion than those who were able to dismiss the whole Nature school with contempt as "pampered humbugs." Delacroix could see that Corot was not "only a man of landscapes" but "a rare genius," and he was not alone. Every year, as one masterpiece after another appeared at the Salon from the "mud-dauber's" brush, the general body of artists and art-lovers were more disposed to give him the rank that was his due.

In 1848 Corot was elected one of the judges for the annual exhibition by his fellow-artists. He himself sent nine pictures, and one of them, a "Site d'Italie," was purchased by the State. The following year Corot was again one of the judges, and in 1850 he was elected a member of the "Jury de Peinture." He had become a personage in the art-world of France. Already in 1846 he had been decorated with the Cross of the Legion of Honour, to the astonishment of his worthy father, who could not in the least understand on what grounds such an honour had been done to his failure of a son.

The history of Corot's following years there is no necessity to follow in detail. Like the years which had gone before, they were fulfilled with happy labour. He journeyed through the length and breadth of France, to Switzerland, and elsewhere, "finding landscapes" with that apprehensive eye of his, and recording them on canvas or on paper, or storing them in the pigeon-holes of a memory that in such matters never failed him. For the rest the record is one of a continually increasing appreciation of his work. It started in a very small circle, extending thence in ever-widening ripples. Almost imperceptibly his fame increased until he became an acknowledged master.

In view of the sums paid for many of them since, the prices he obtained for his pictures seem ridiculously small, but there is no reason to suppose that he was anything but well content with such material rewards as came his way. Indeed, so much to the contrary, for some time he looked upon the increasing prices which purchasers were willing to pay with a mild astonishment and a kind of humorous fear that it was too good to be true.

The slighting of his earlier work and the laudation excited by the later had precisely the same effect upon him – that is none at all. If one had asked him, I think he would have said both alike were out of perspective. And he would have spoken without any taint of bitterness: for, from the very first, he was both confident and humble.

Of the man Corot there are many portraits both in pen and pencil, that help to give an outward shape to the more intimate revelation of personality to be found in his work.

One of the most interesting is a portrait by the artist of himself as a young man. He is sitting, a burly, broad-shouldered figure, before his easel. The face looks out from the canvas square and strong, but the full-lipped mouth is sensitive, almost tremulous, and betrays the nature of the man even more surely than the alert eyes; though these eyes, on the pounce, one may say, and the forehead drawn in the intense endeavour to *see* – these also tell their own story.

A pen-portrait of later date by Silvestre describes the artist as "of short but Herculean build; his chest and shoulders are solid as an iron chest; his large and powerful hands could throw the ordinary strong man out of the window. Attacked once, when with Marilhat, by a band of peasants of the Midi, he knocked down the most energetic of them with a single blow, and afterwards, gentle again and sorry, he said, 'It is astonishing; I did not know I was so strong.' He is very full-blooded, and his face of a high colour. This, with the bourgeois cut of his clothes and the plebeian shape of his shoes, gives him at first sight a look which disappears in a conversation that is nearly always full of point, of wit, and matter. He explains his principles with great ease, and illustrates the method of his art with anything at hand; and that generally is his pipe. He so loves to talk about his practices in painting that, a student told me, he will talk in his shorts and with bare feet for two hours at a stretch without being once distracted by the cold."

Many photographs are in existence to present to us Corot in his autumn time. Says M. Gustave Geffroy, examining one of these: "The features are clearly marked. The brow, high and bare, crowned with hair in the *coup de vent* style, is furrowed with lines. His glance goes clear, keen, direct, from beneath the heavy eyelids. The nose, short and fleshy, is attached to the cheeks by two strongly marked creases. There is a smile on the lips, of which the lower is very thick – altogether a good, intelligent, witty face." In general appearance, I may add, these later portraits of Corot always remind me of the late Mr. Lionel Brough.

To my mind there is something more in these photographs than M. Geffroy has called attention to. They are the portraits of a very happy man. A deep spiritual happiness and content make the old, wrinkled face a beautiful one. It is the face of one who, to use a lovely old phrase, "walked with God," and of whom it was said, "*c'est le Saint Vincent de Paul de la peinture*."

As one of his friends said, Corot was "adorably good." He was a good son, for all that he found himself unable to fall in with his father's desire to make him a successful draper: and the fact that "at home" his outstanding abilities were never recognised, could not in the least abate the warmth of his family affections. And he was a good friend. He never forgot a kindness done to him either in word or deed, although his memory seemed to be singularly incapable of retaining a record of anything done to his hurt. It has been said, and the argument could be powerfully supported, that the same qualities that go to the making of a good friend make a bad enemy. Very likely it is true in ninety-nine cases out of a hundred: if so the case of Corot was the hundredth. He seemed to have a natural incapacity to bear malice or retain a sense of injury. Perhaps he was too simple or too wise; or, maybe, both.

Not less characteristic of Corot than his manner of going about always with a song on his lips, was his incurable habit of giving. The wonder is that he ever had anything at all left for himself, that even shoes and soup did not follow after francs. And very reprehensibly, of course, he gave to almost every one who had recourse to him, as well as to many who did not. His generosity was all but indiscriminate, and conducted in a manner that, it may be supposed, would drive a charity organisation society to distraction. He was victimised often and knew it, but the knowledge never dulled the edge of an insatiable appetite. To give was at once a luxury and a necessity to him, as appears, and he was never so gay as when he had been indulging himself in this direction rather more recklessly than usual. "He would paint" (I quote from Meynell), "saying to himself, 'Now I am making twice what I have just given.' Or, again, having just emptied his cash drawer, he would take up his easel, saying: 'Now we will paint great pictures. Now we will surprise the nations.'" Rather a foolish fellow evidently: but "one of God's fools," as I heard an old priest say of a somewhat similar example.

Notwithstanding the love that made the keynote of his character, all the investigations of the curious have not discovered an "affair of the heart" in Corot's life story. It is a story to all intents and purposes without a woman in it: or, if that is saying too much, certainly without a heroine. There has been some attempt to exalt his relations with "Mademoiselle Rose" to the level of a romance, but it has failed completely for want of materials. Mademoiselle Rose was one of his mother's work girls, and in those early days, when he was but newly emancipated from the bondage of drapery, she used to come to see him at his painter-work. She never married, and thirty-five years later Corot still counted her among his friends, and she visited him from time to time. It is a little romance of friendship, if you like, it may have been on the part of Mademoiselle Rose something more – who knows? – but it cannot count as a Corot love-affair on the evidence that is available.

As far as is known this is the nearest approach to a "love interest" in the life of the artist. It may have been that he looked upon women too much with the eye of an artist ever to be able to see them merely as a man; more probably it was the element of austerity in him that kept him immune from passion.

With all his intense delight in life and in living, Corot was always detached; always preserved, as by a religious habit, from actual contact with the world around him. Through the midst of the follies, the extravagances, and the vices of Romanticist circles in Paris of the thirties, he passed without coming to any harm, and characteristically enough, without losing his regard for some of the wildest of a wild company. He took part in much of the "fun" that was going on, but though often in the set he was never of it, and so far as can be judged it did not influence him, or colour his outlook upon life, in the slightest degree.

I think it was this temperamental detachment, and possibly a sense, unexpressed even to himself, of being vowed to one particular service, that prevented Corot from ever "falling in love," as the phrase goes. Or, to put it another way, his life was so full of his art, that there was no room within its limits for another dominating interest.

Simple and single-minded, happily pursuing the occupation that of all others he would have chosen, he made his life a work of art more lovely than the most beautiful of his paintings. No one can live in such a world as this for the allotted span and more without becoming acquainted with grief, but Corot knew none of those searing sorrows which scorch their way into heart and brain, until they make existence a burden hardly to be borne. His faith in "the good God," to whom he looked up with so childlike a confidence, was so complete that sorrow for him could hold no bitterness; nor, deeply sympathetic as he was, had it power over an impregnable content and an unfailing serenity.

And he died as he had lived. A few days before his death it is recorded "that he told one of his friends how in a dream he had seen 'a landscape with a sky all roses, and clouds all roses too. It was delicious,' he said; 'I can remember it quite well. It will be an admirable thing to paint.' The morning of the day he died, the 22nd of February, 1875, he said to the woman servant who brought him some nourishment, 'Le père Corot is lunching up there to-day.'"

> "It will be hard to replace the artist; the man can never be replaced," was one fine tribute to his memory; and another, "Death might have had pity and paused before cutting short so sweet a life-work."

A sale of some 600 of Corot's works took place in the May and June following his death. It realised nearly two million francs, or £80,000. This is, of course, not a fraction of the sum that would be realised were the same pictures to be put up to auction to-day; but it shows that his achievement was beginning to be estimated at something approaching its true value.

Corot's work, of which at one time he was able to boast he had a "complete collection," is now scattered to the four corners of the earth. Paris possesses some splendid examples at the Louvre, and there are many not less admirable distributed among the provincial galleries of France. America holds a large number in public and private galleries, and there are in private ownership in this country Corots sufficient to make a magnificent collection. Lately the National Gallery has been enriched, by the Salting bequest, with seven fine paintings from the master's hand, eloquent witnesses alike to his individuality and variety.

To me it is an added joy, when I stand before a Corot picture, to think of the gracious personality of its creator. It is almost as if his eager, happy voice were pointing out the manifold beauties of the miraculously bedaubed canvas, and recalling the "moment," so certainly made permanent there.

It is always a "moment" that is seized in Corot's paintings, with the exception of some of the earliest. Nature is surprised with her fairest charms unveiled, in a passing emotion, of laughter or of tears. There is life, movement, the tremble of being, in everything set down. The air is palpitant with colour, rainbows are dissolved in an atmosphere that clothes everything in magic and mystery.

Beneath the gay confidence of the painting, subserving the emotion of the moment, what knowledge is shown in these pictures! These tree forms, bold and delicate, with such wonderful subtleties of drawing in them, give more than externals. They reveal a very psychology of trees, the soul that the artist so plainly saw in everything around him. He was concerned to set down far more than the details of the scene before him, not in the least satisfied to be but a reporter. The higher, or, if you like, deeper verities were what he strove for, and the universal verdict to-day is that he did not strive in vain.

The figure-painting of Corot is comparatively little known, and it is a subject of too much importance to attempt to deal with adequately in small space. An enthusiastic critic claims that it includes the artist's "absolute masterpieces," but I doubt if many would agree, beautiful as some of these figures are. They show the same faculty of apprehending a sudden revelation of beauty as is shown by the more familiar landscapes, the same exquisite sense of graces in form and colour, which elude the eyes of most of us. But it is still in landscape that Corot is supreme.

I have already stated my conviction that he was not greatly influenced by other artists, his predecessors, or contemporaries. Perhaps Constable, to mention but one name, helped to open his eyes, but once open he used them as his own. Again, the classicism which surrounded him in his youth left gentle memories that in his age were never quite forgotten; but it was worn as sometimes an elderly gentleman wears a bunch of seals, and had about as much to do with the essential personality of the wearer.

He was always true to himself. His equipment was simple faith, definite purpose, and unflagging zeal. A clear eye, a dream-haunted brain, and a great loving heart – that was Corot.

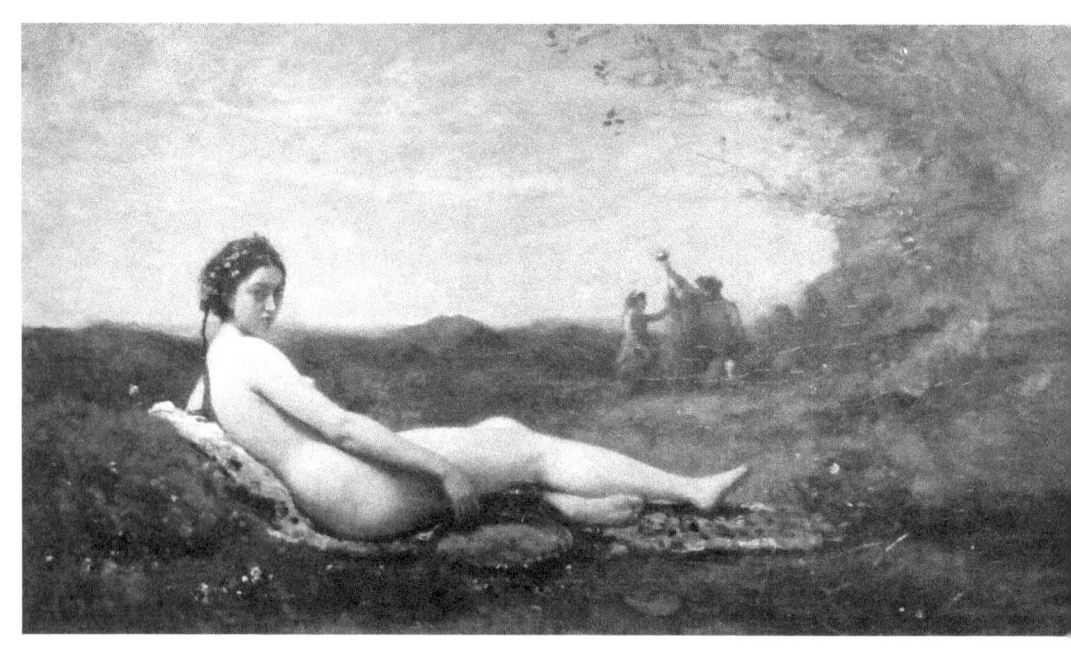

J.B.C. Corot, Repose, 1860-70, Corcoran Gallery of Art

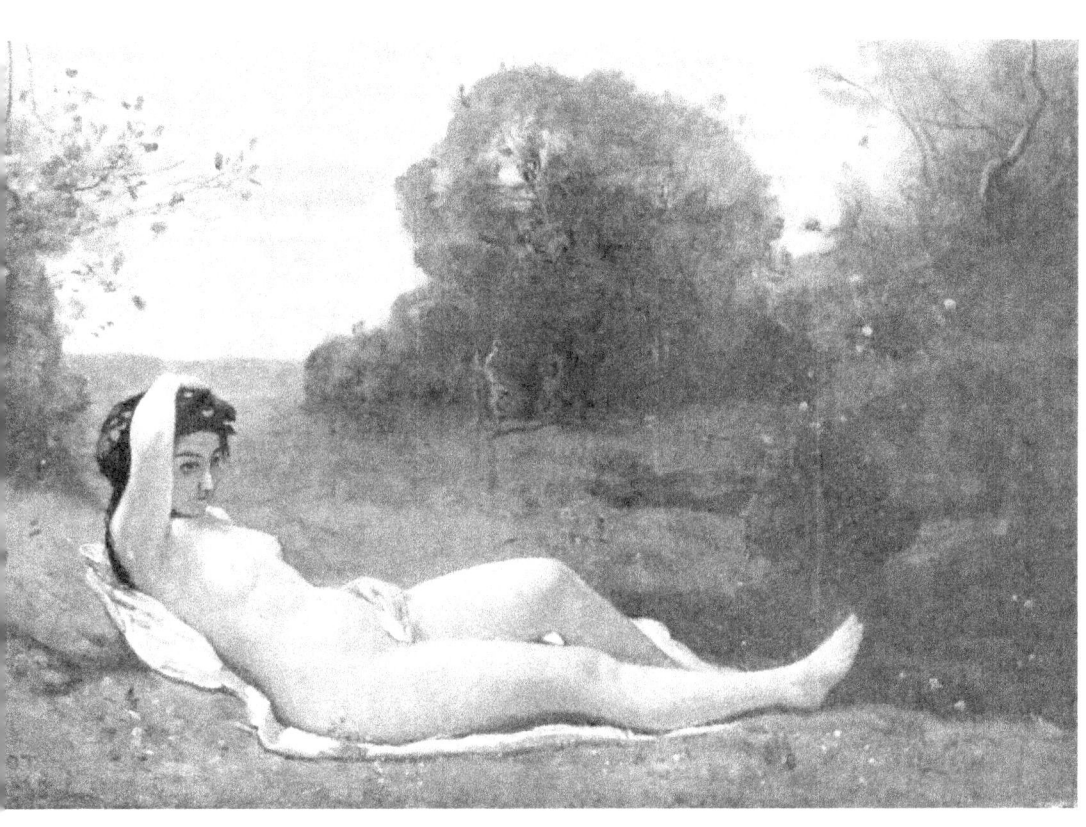

J.B.C. Corot, Jeune fille en vert, 1859, Geneva

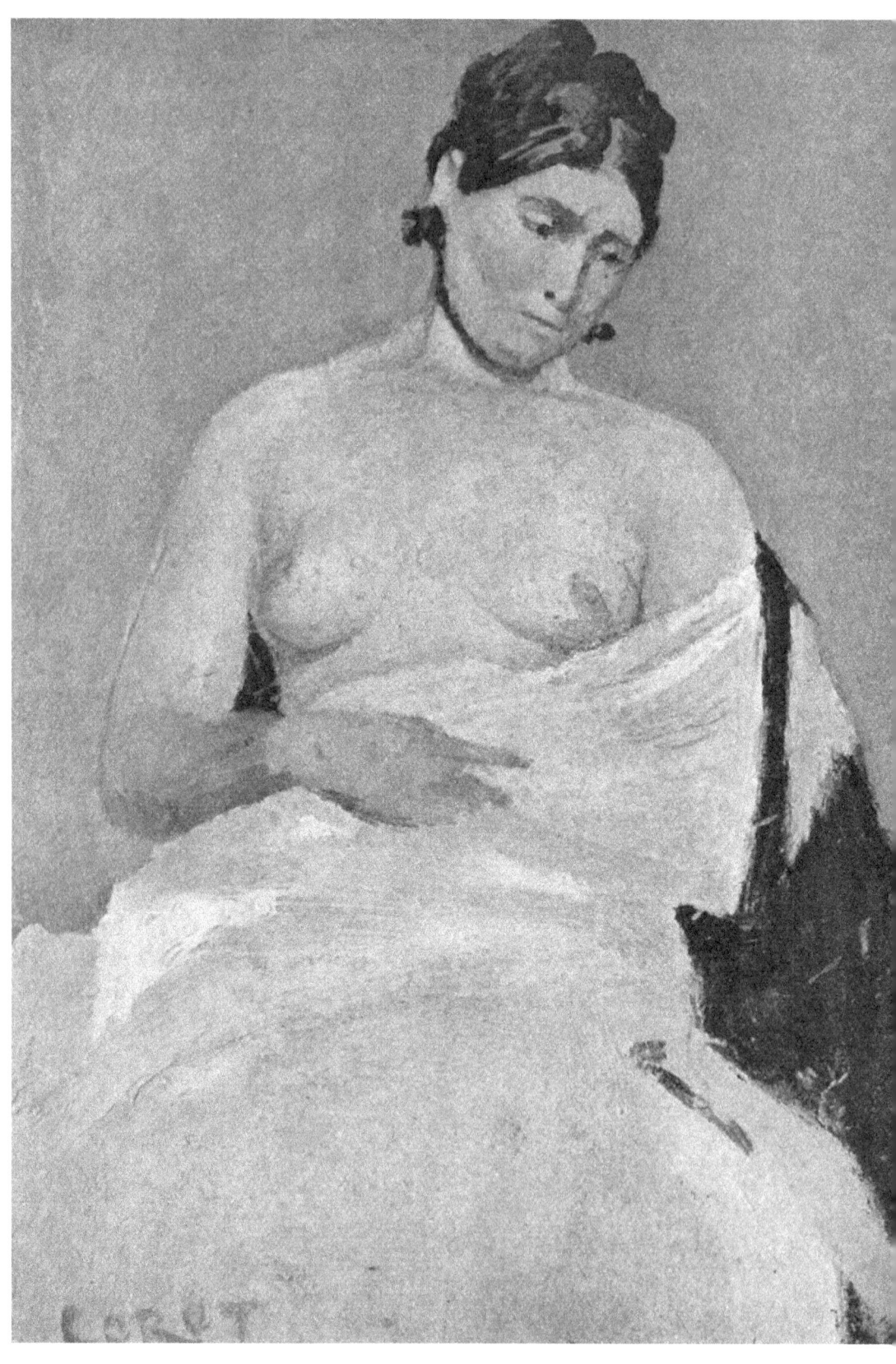

J.B.C. Corot, Seated Woman With Bare Bosom, 1835, Paris

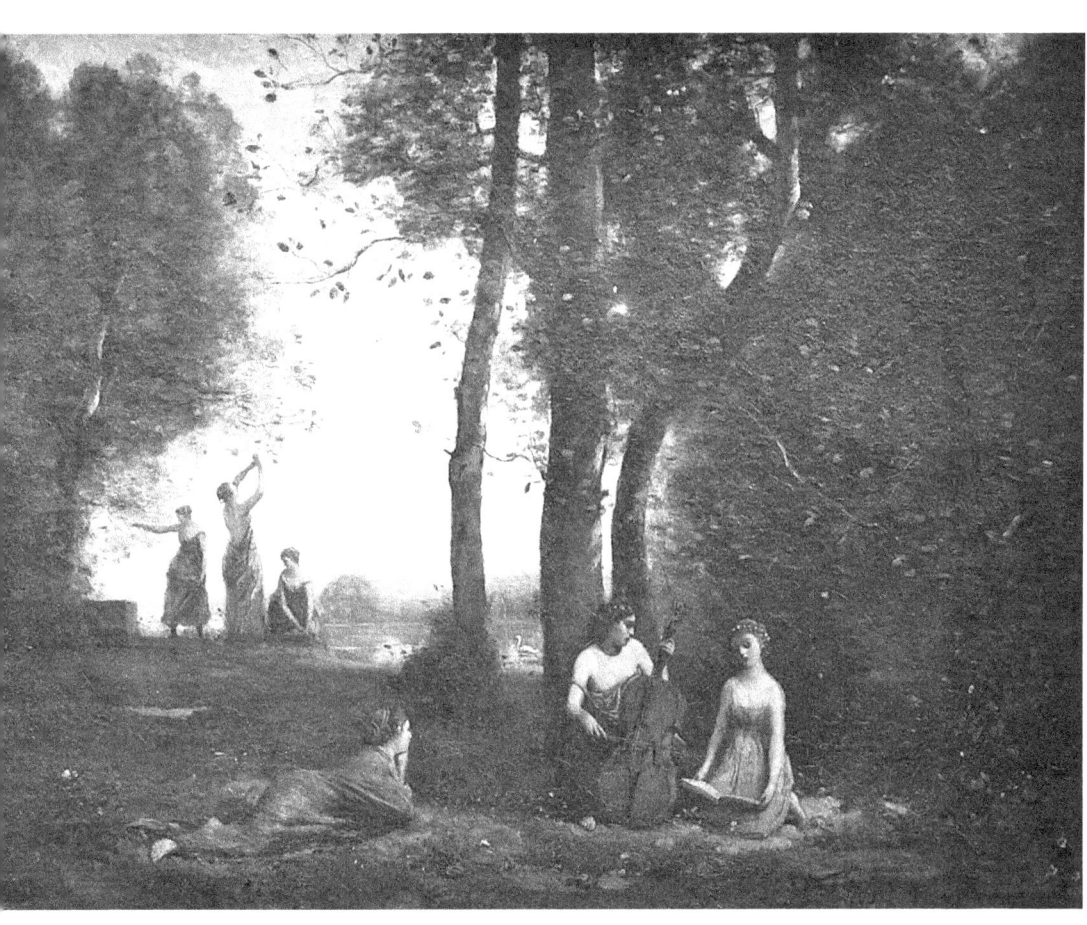

J.B.C. Corot, Concert Champêtre Condé Chantilly, 1857, Chantilly

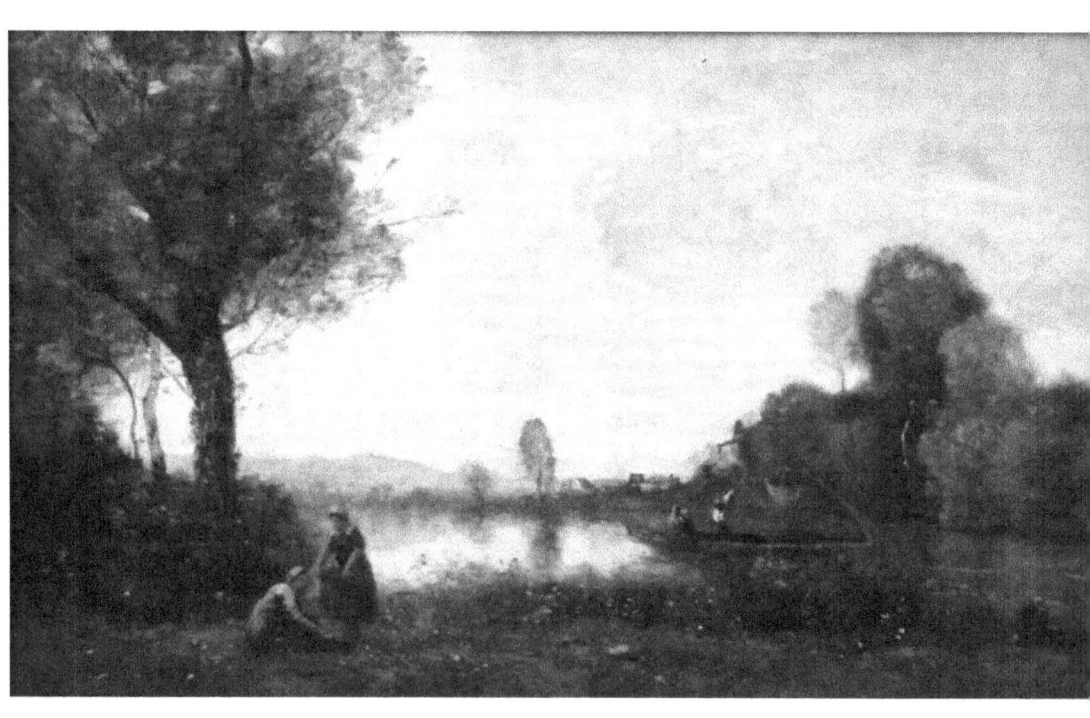

J.B.C. Corot, Seinelandschaft bei Chatou, 1855, Berlin

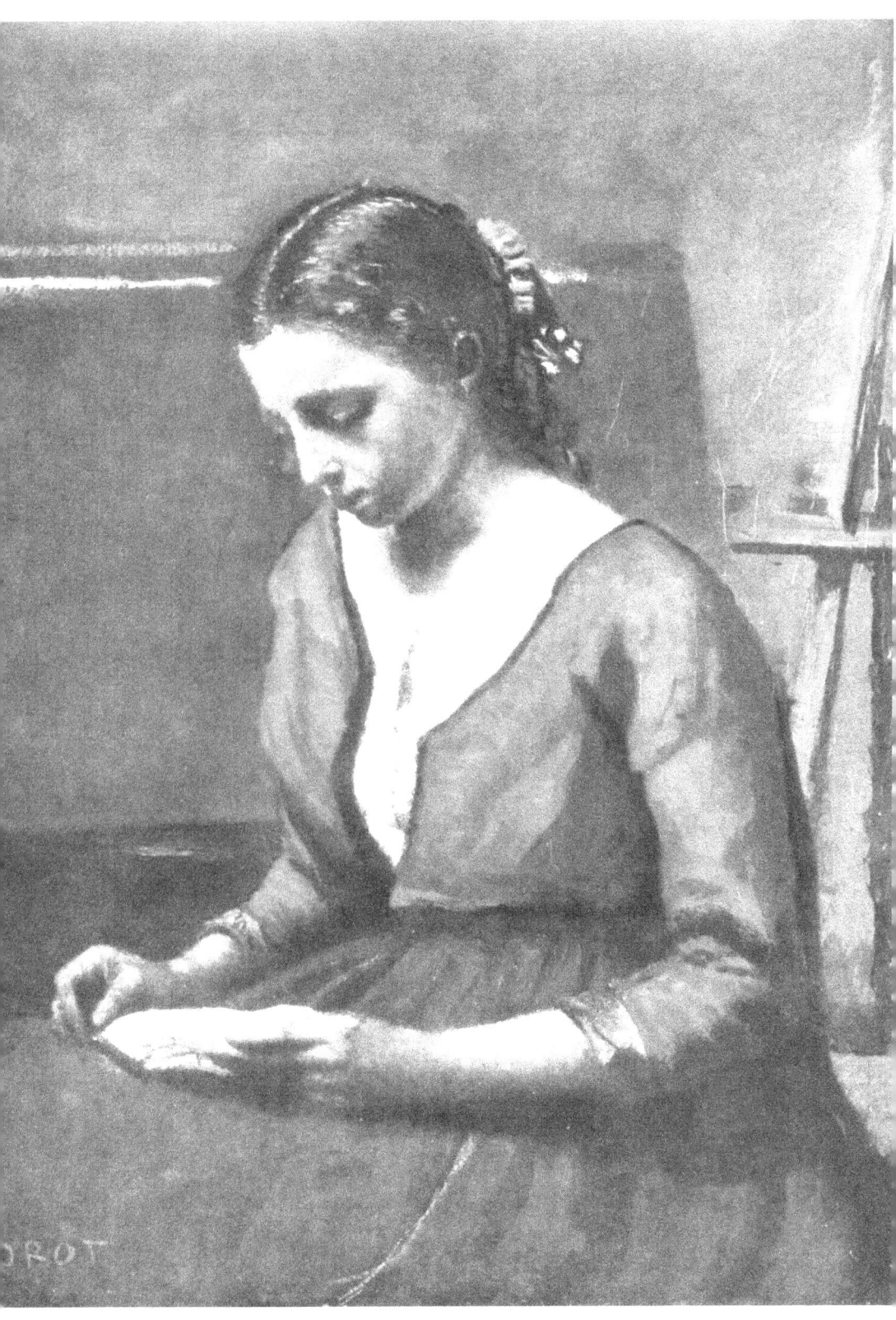

J.B.C. Corot, Young Woman Reading, 1845-50, Zurich

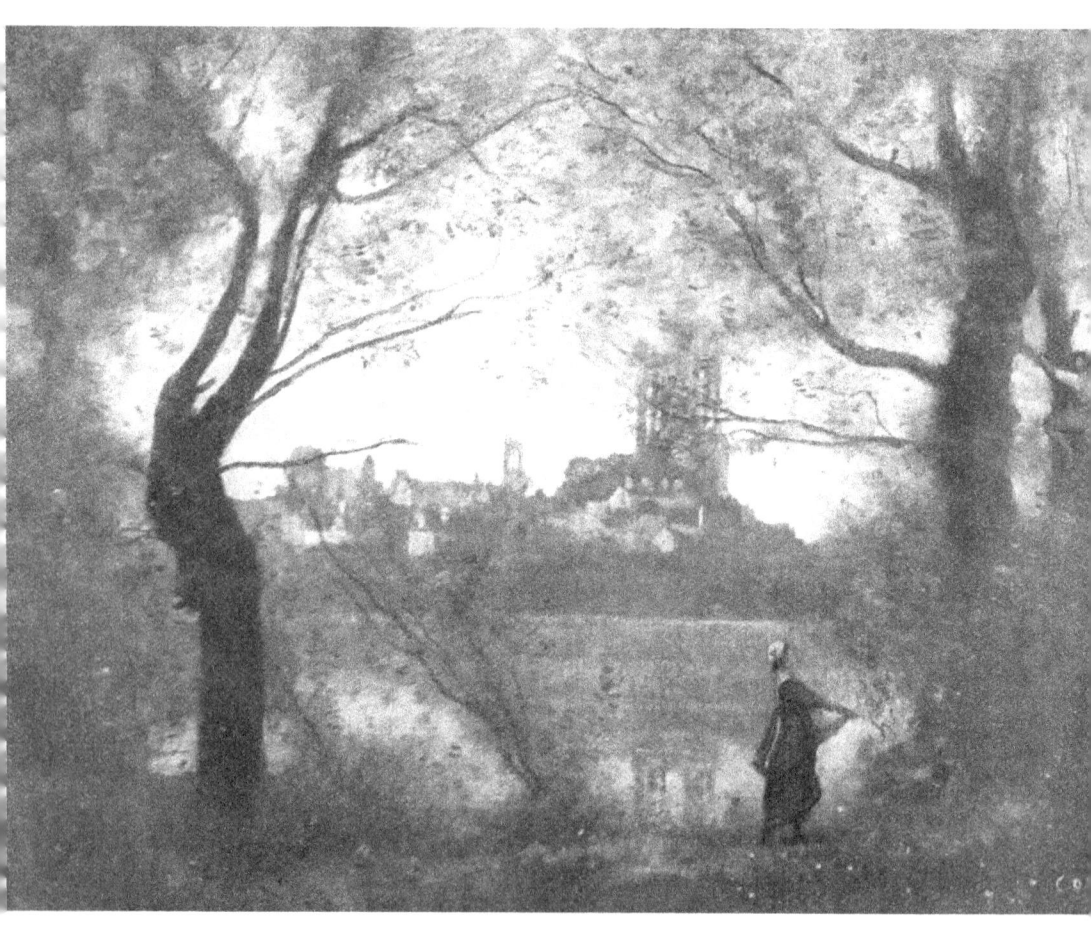

J.B.C. Corot, Cathedral of Mantes, Wth Young Woman, 1860, Rheims

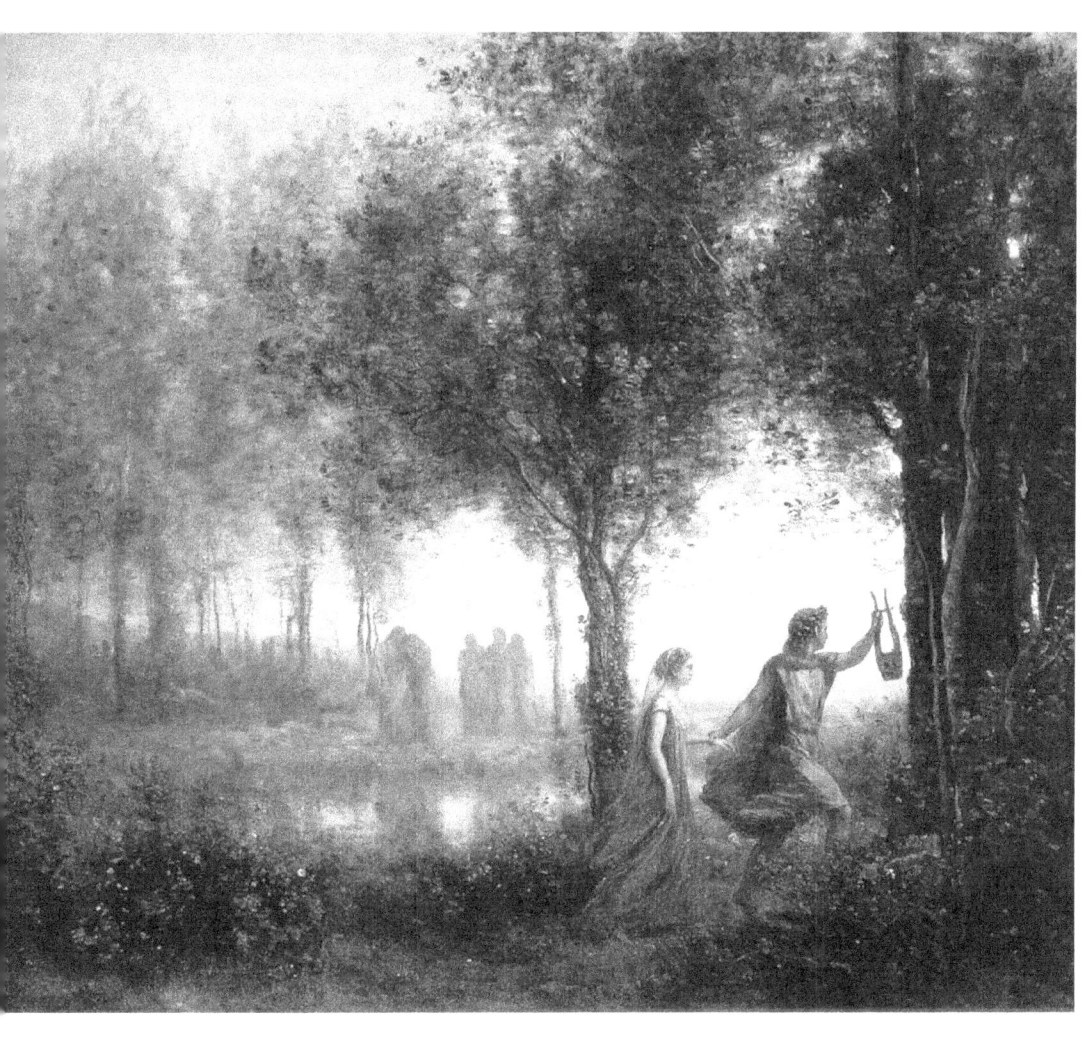

J.B.C. Corot, Orpheus, 1861, Houston, TX

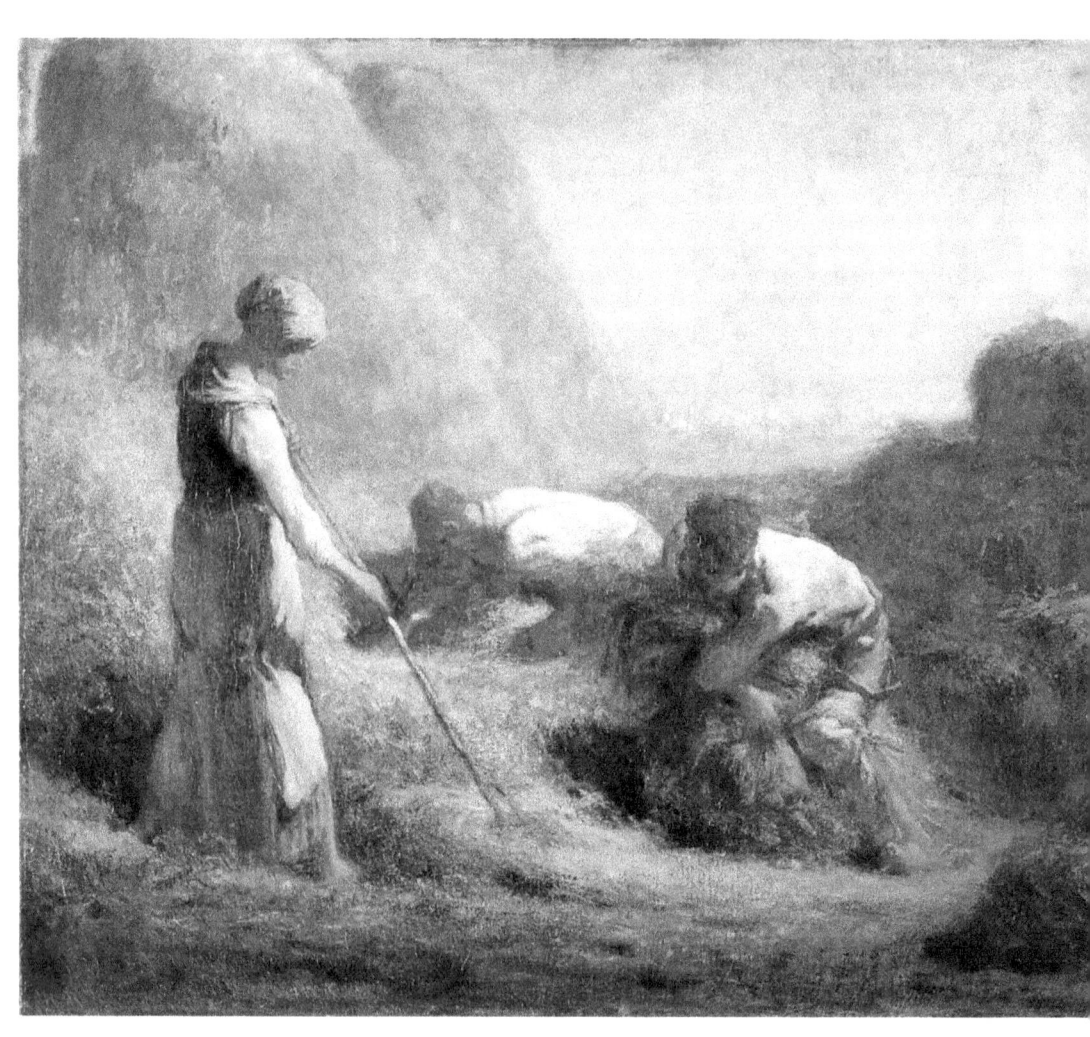

J.B.C. Corot, The Haymakers, 1850-51

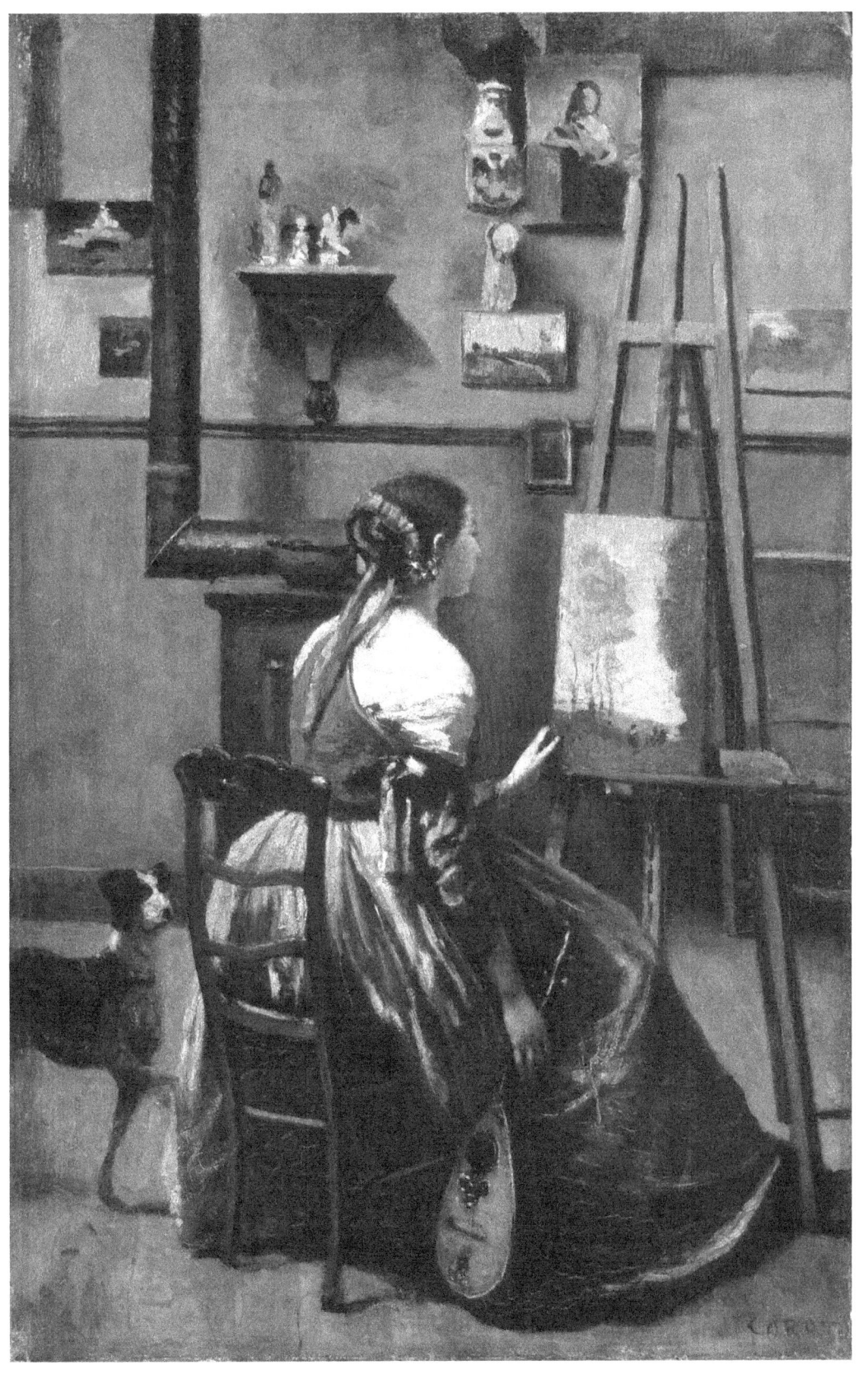

J.B.C. Corot, The Artist's Studio, c. 1868, Washington, DC

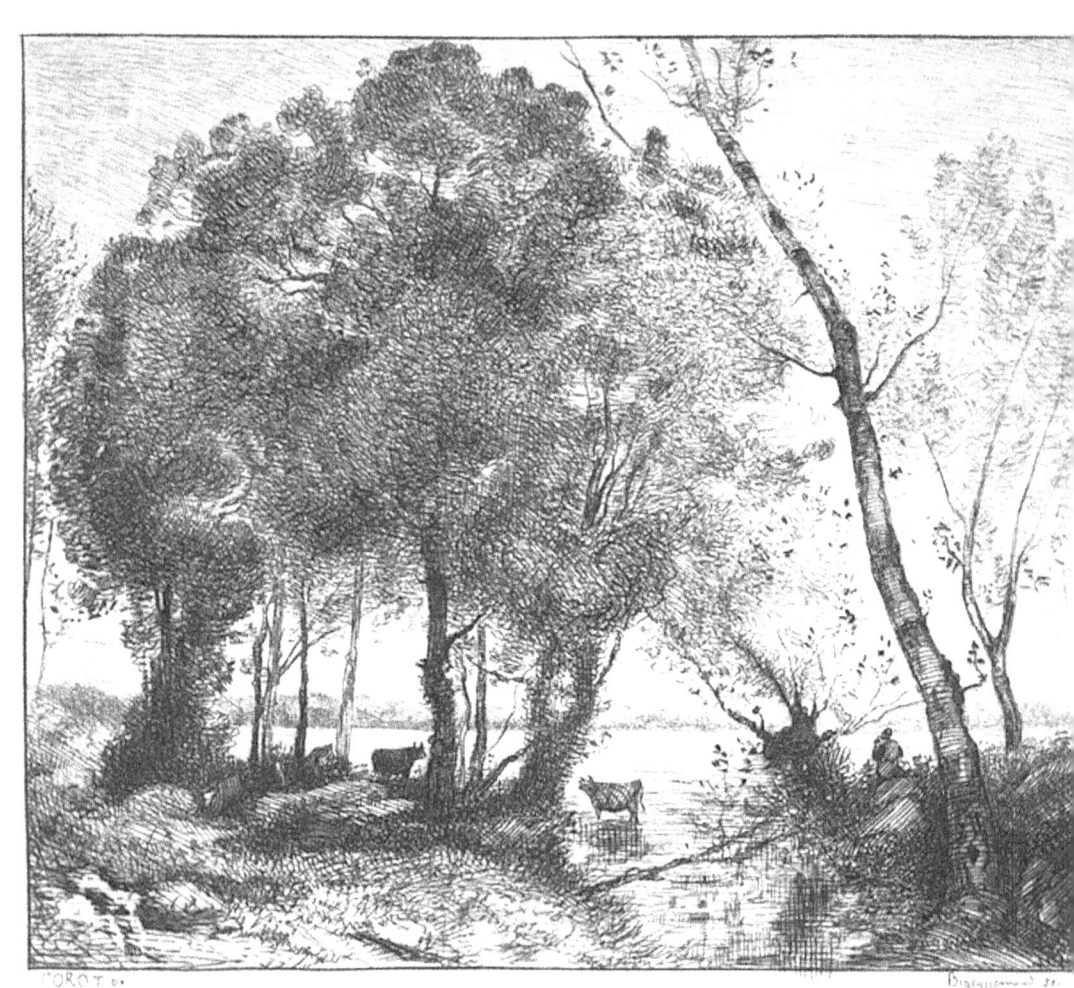

After Corot, The Lake, Metropolitan Museum of Art, NYC

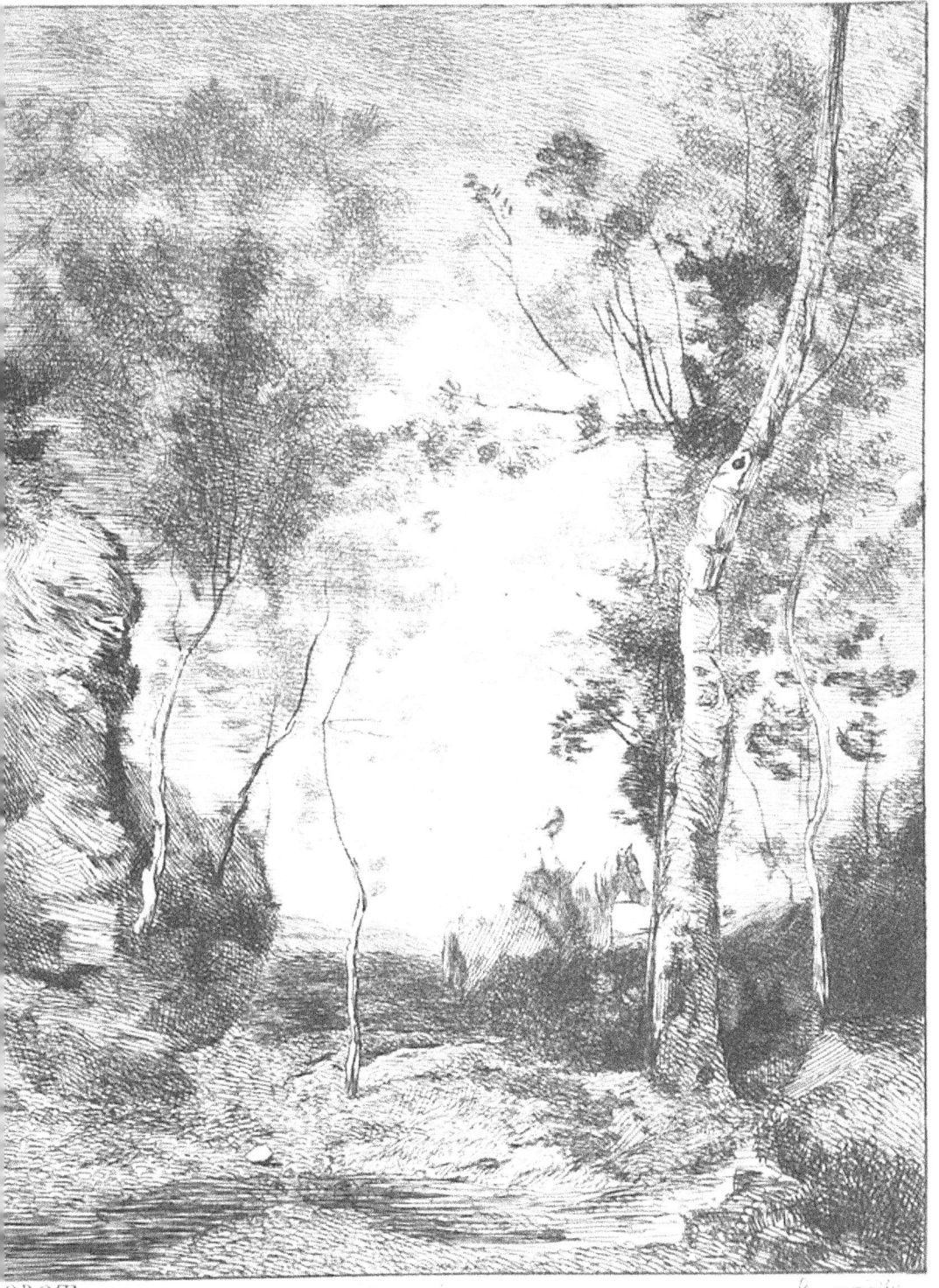

OROT.

After Corot, The White Horse, Metropolitan Museum of Art, NYC

NOTES ON WORKS

DANSE DES BERGERS.

The "Danse des Bergers" is the living memorial of a happy mood – one of those moments of lyrical ecstasy of which Corot experienced so many, and which, by his genius, those less fortunate are enabled to share. The "feeling" in the drawing and painting of the trees is reminiscent of some words spoken by the painter when Paris was oppressing him – "I need living boughs. I want to see how the leaves of the willow grow from their branches. I am going to the country. When I bury my nose in a hazel-bush, I shall be fifteen years old. It is good; it breathes love!"

L'ETANG.

"Beauty in art is truth bathed in the impression, the emotion that is received from nature.... Seek truth and exactitude, but with the envelope of sentiment which you felt at first. If you have been sincere in your emotion you will be able to pass it on to others." So said Corot to a pupil, and "L'Etang" would in itself be sufficient to prove that he knew how to practise what he preached.

It is a variant on a simple motive that he was never weary of, and that he knew how to invest with new beauties every time it came to him.

LES CHAUMIÈRES

Luminous and almost uncannily true in tone, "Les Chaumières" takes high rank among the finest productions of Corot's maturer years. It is the work of a man who "knows," who is able to take hold of essentials, and let non-essentials go, with a certainty of discrimination. Profound knowledge, so thoroughly assimilated as to be instinctive in its application, can alone account for both the completeness and simplicity of the landscape, the result achieved with apparently so absolute a lack of effort.

LE SOIR

"My 'Soir,' I love it, I love it! It is so firm," said Corot, standing before his picture in the exhibition gallery in company with an appreciative friend. It is "firm" enough beyond question, and the sky especially is a marvel of delicate, palpitating colour. But it is much more, a moment of magic beauty, evanescent as the reflected picture on a bubble-bell, seized and made permanent; an emotion of pleasure cast into a material shape.

PAYSAGE

The play of light filtering through foliage has never been more beautifully rendered upon canvas, or with a closer approximation to the truth of Nature, than in the "Paysage," reproduced here. The manner in which the tree has been portrayed, the body and soul of it, is not less astonishing. The landscape is a masterpiece among masterpieces, and an impressive witness to Corot's amazingly sensitive faculty of apprehending what was in front of him, both with eye and mind.

LE VALLON

"Le Vallon" is probably one of the best-known and most universally admired of Corot's works. It does not record one of those tender twilight effects in which, as may be believed, the painter found his keenest pleasure, but the quiet glory of a golden afternoon. The simple landscape is bathed in the most wonderful of painted sunshine, and possesses an extraordinary verity. The material essentials of the scene are set down with an unerring regard for truth, but it is in interpreting its "sentiment" that the most notable success has been achieved.

SOUVENIR D'ITALIE

Corot at the height of his powers is seen in the "Souvenir d'Italie." The thousand subtle nuances of exquisite colour in the luminous sky, the refined drawing and firm painting of the trees, and the happy confidence revealed by every brush mark upon the canvas, make it one of the most delightful and, we may say, most "lovable" of its creator's works.

VUE DU COLISÉE

The "Vue du Colisée" is a reminiscence of Corot's first visit to Rome. It plainly shows that even in those early days he had obtained a great mastery of his medium, and could set down with distinction what he so clearly saw. Though the subject is a big one, it is handled in such a fashion that simple dignity is its outstanding characteristic. The "Vue du Colisée" was one of the paintings that first gained for Corot the high consideration of the more discerning among his artist friends.

On the following pages are illustrations of some of the contemporaries of Corot.

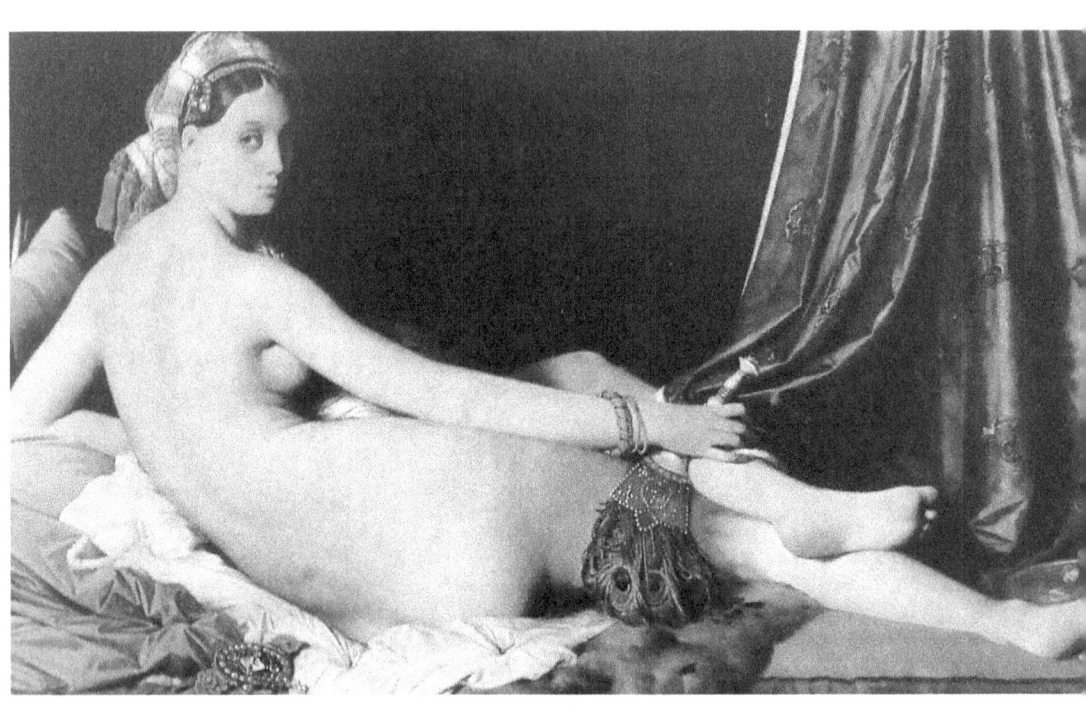

Jean-Dominique Ingres, Grand Odalisque, 1814

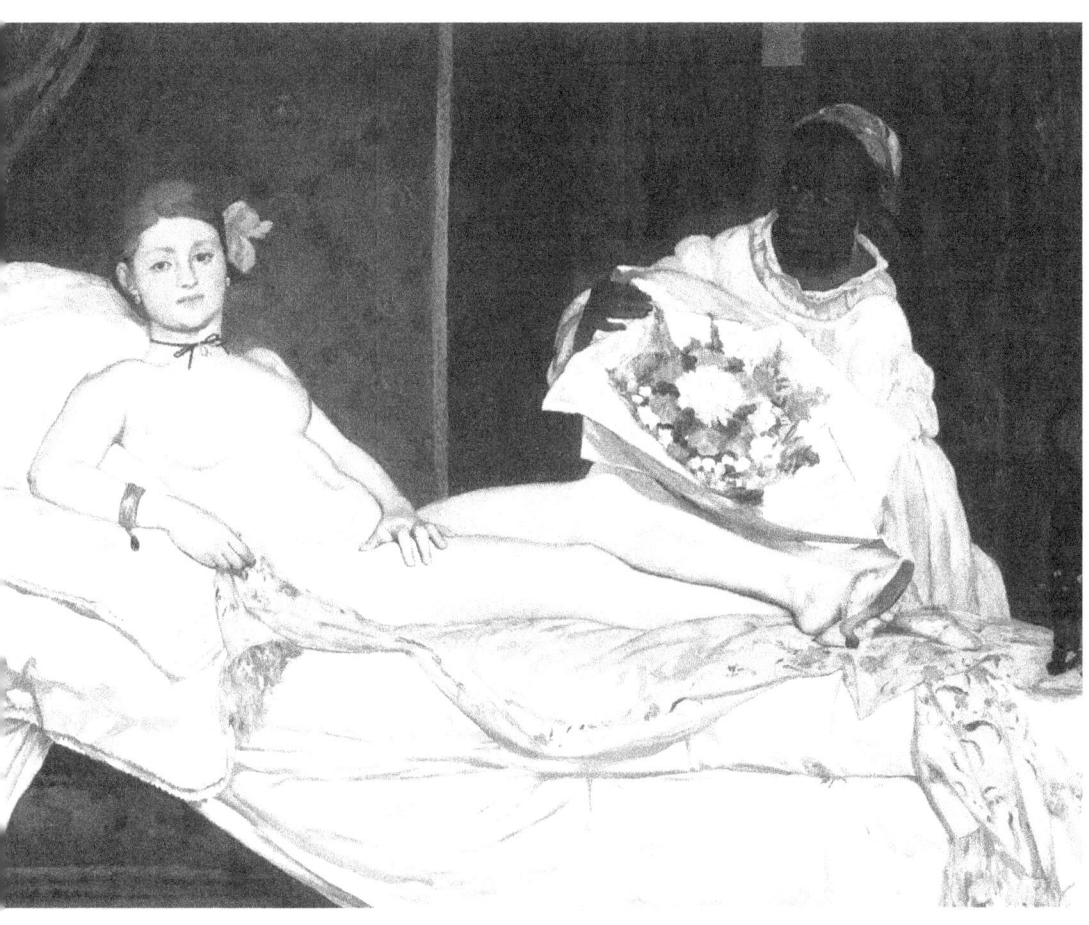

Edouard Manet, Olympia, Musée d'Orsay, Paris

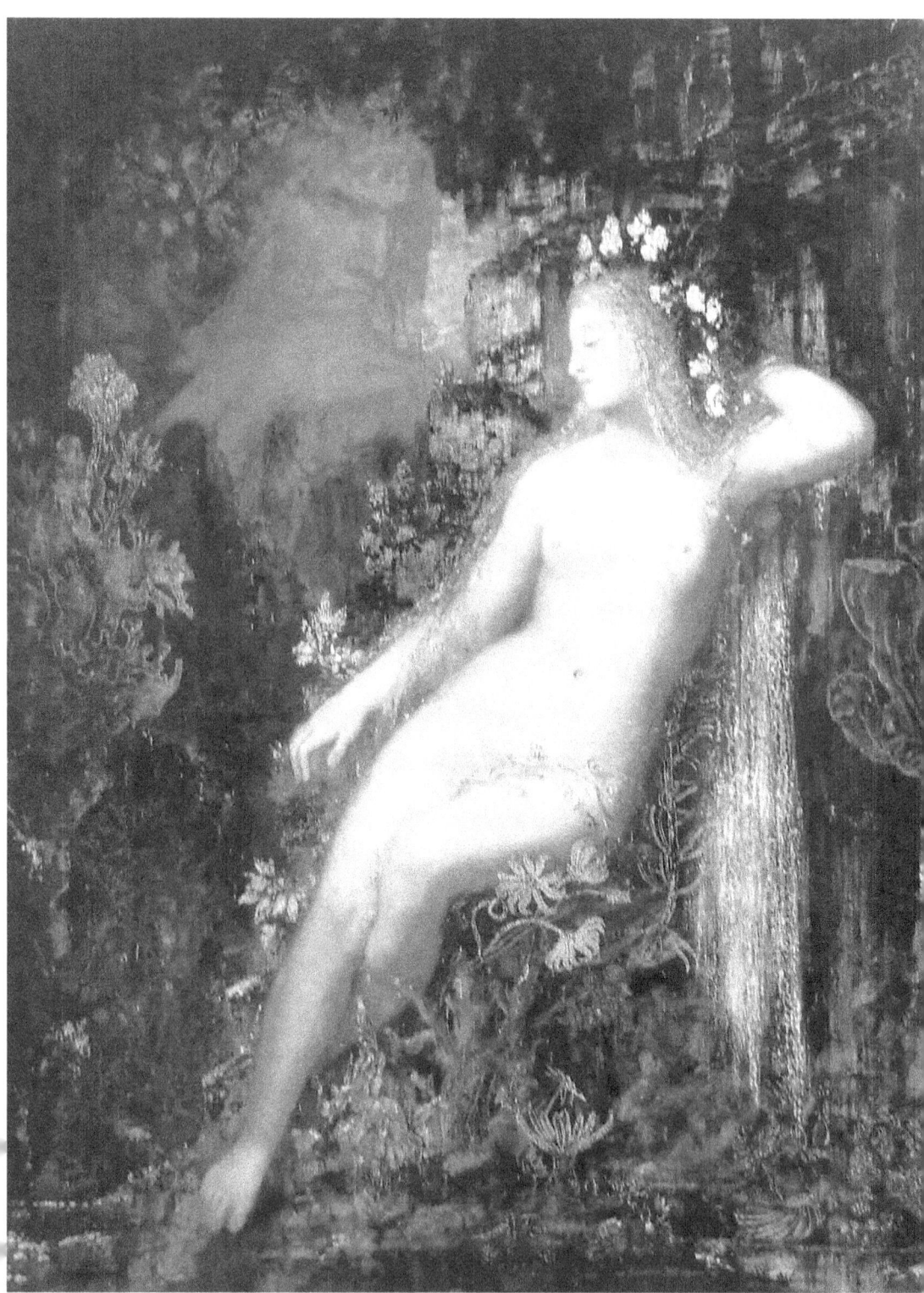

Gustave Moreau, Galatea, 1880

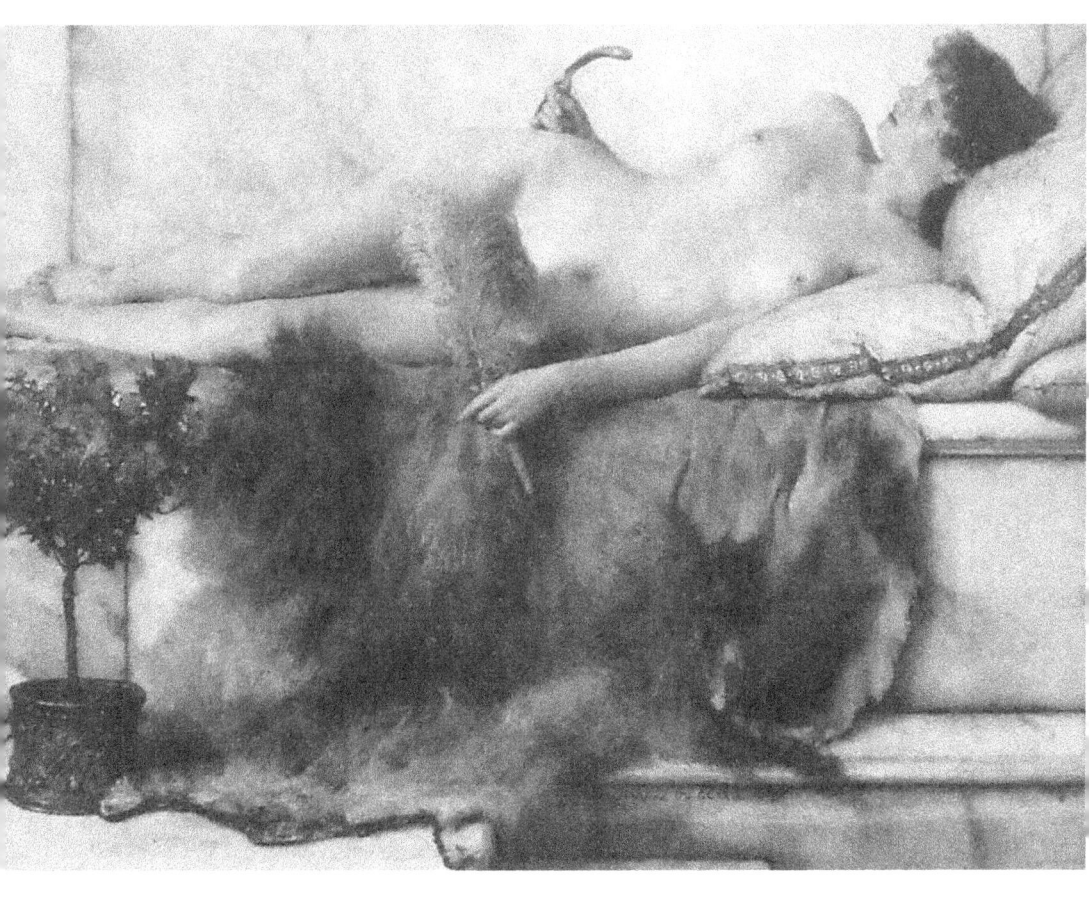

Lawrence Alma-Tadema, In the Tepidarium, 1881,
Lady Lever Art Gallery, Liverpool

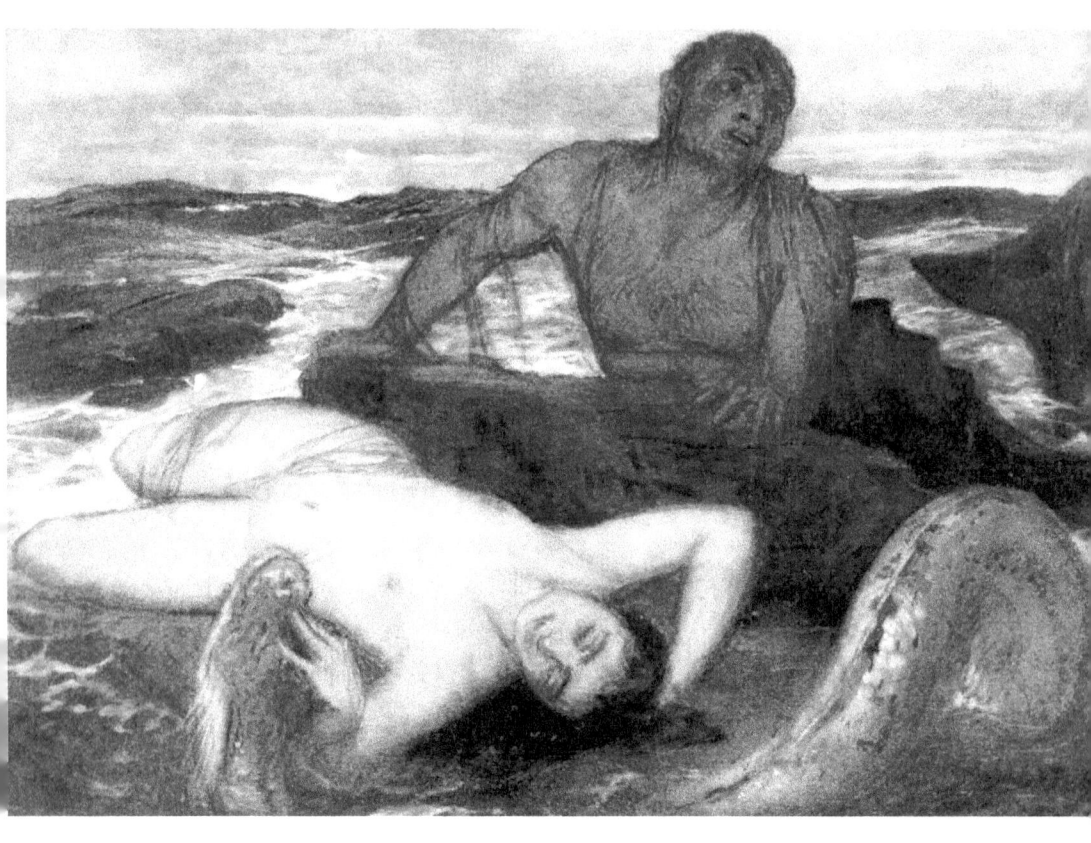

Arnold Böcklin, Triton and Nereid, 1877

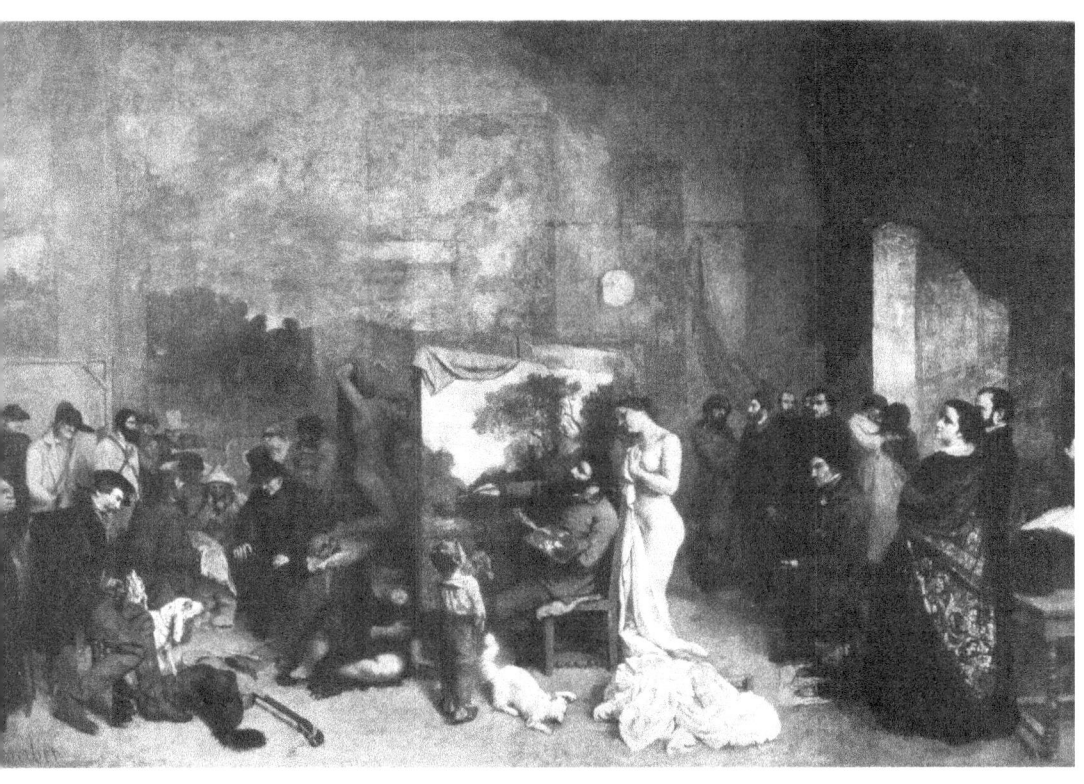

Gustave Courbet, The Studio, 1855, Musée d'Orsay, Paris

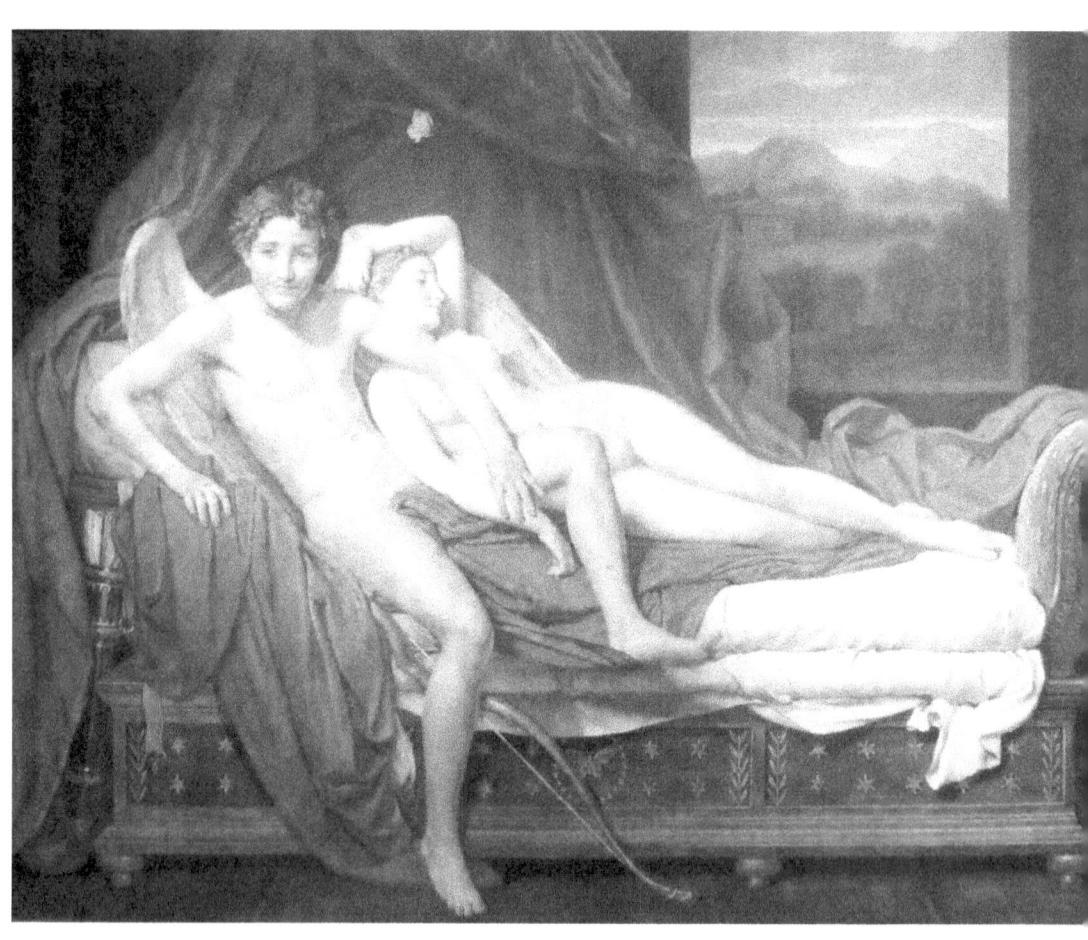

Jacques-Louis David, Cupid and Psyche, 1817,
Cleveland Museum of Art

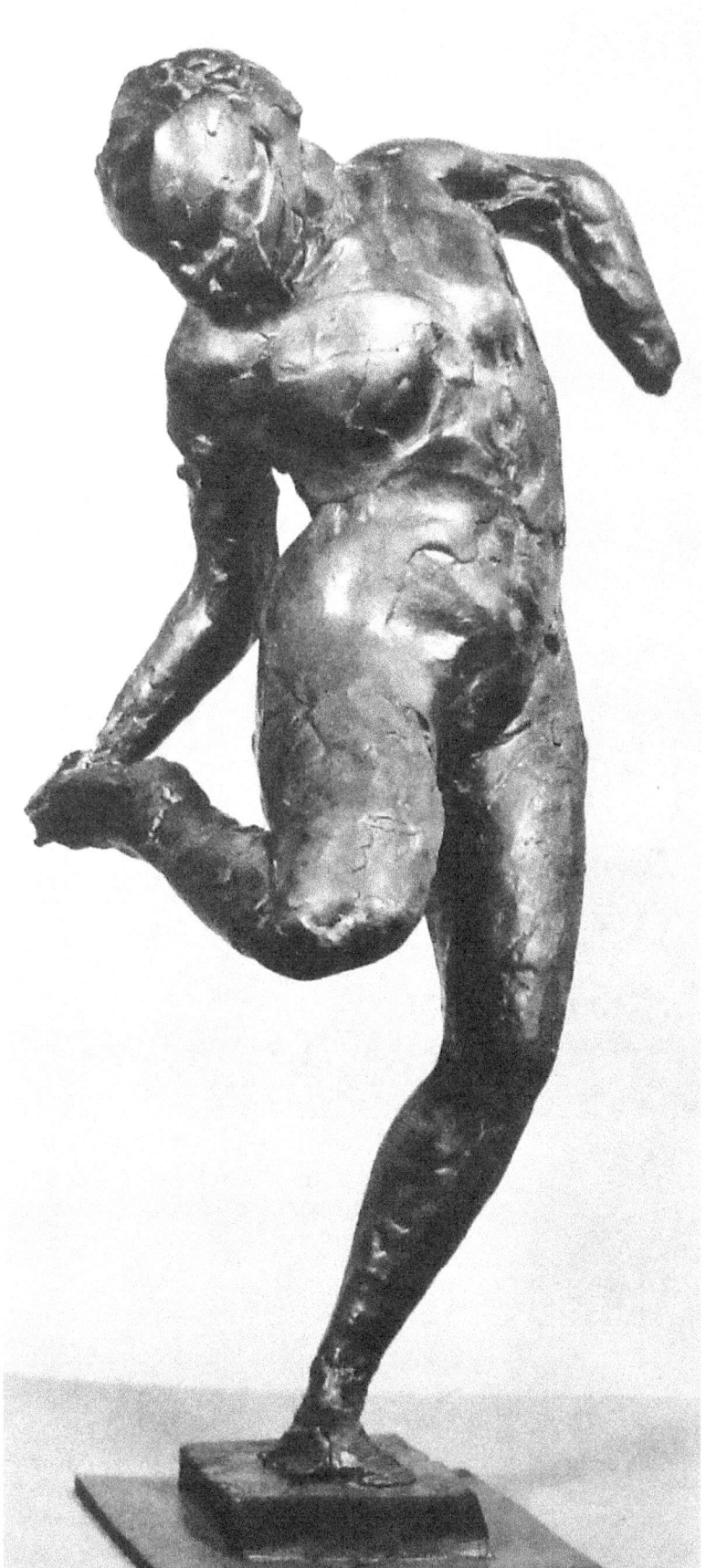

Edgar Degas,
Dancer Looking At
the Sole of Her
Right Foot, 1882-95,
New York

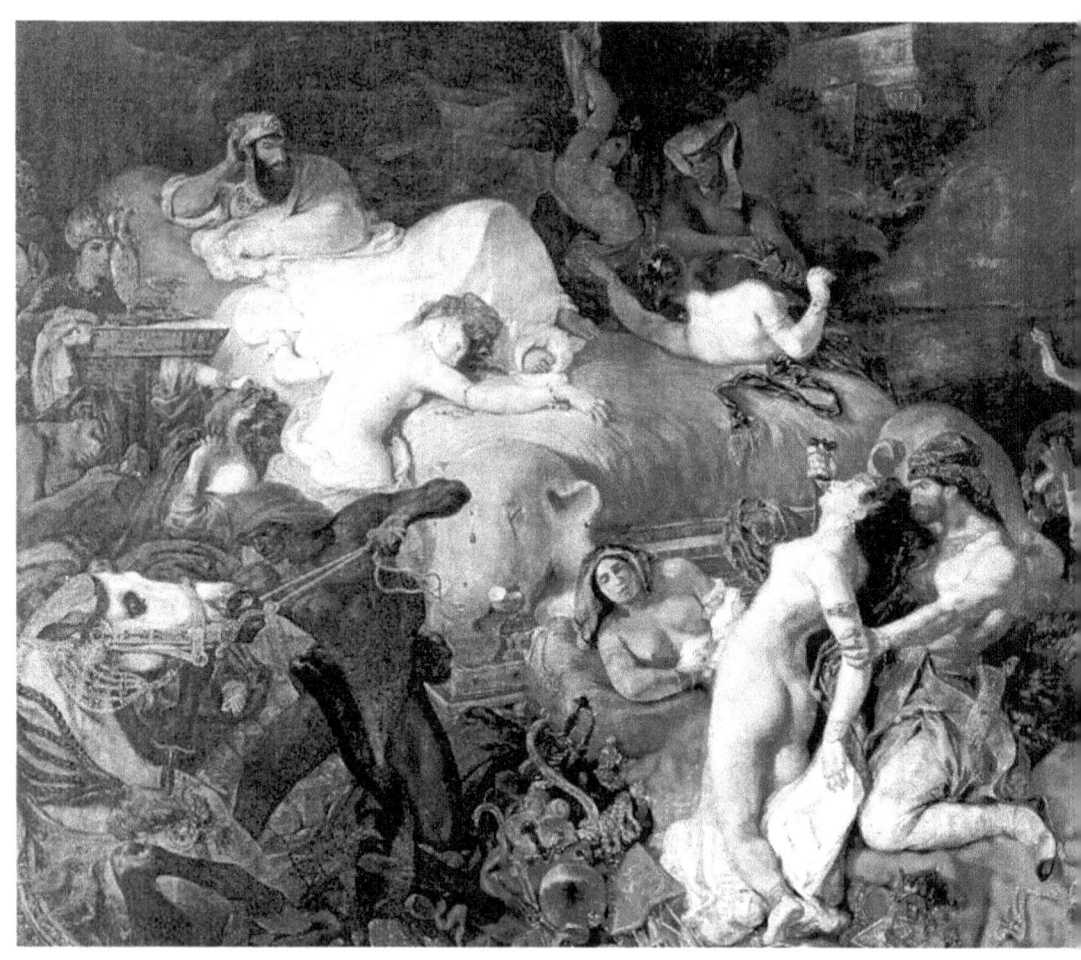

Eugène Delacroix, The Death of Sardanapalus, 1827
(this page and over).

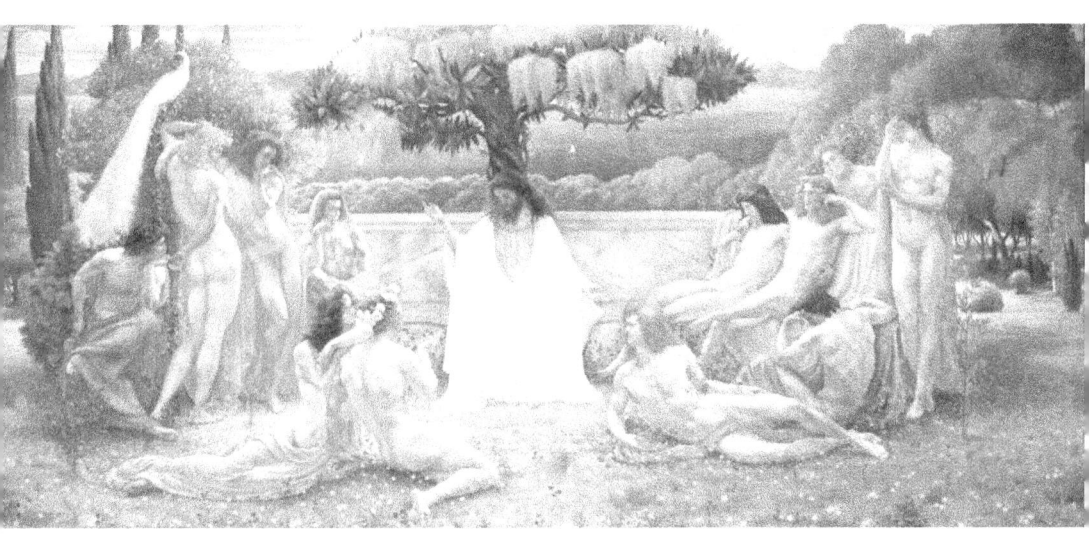

Jean Delville, The School of Plato, 1898

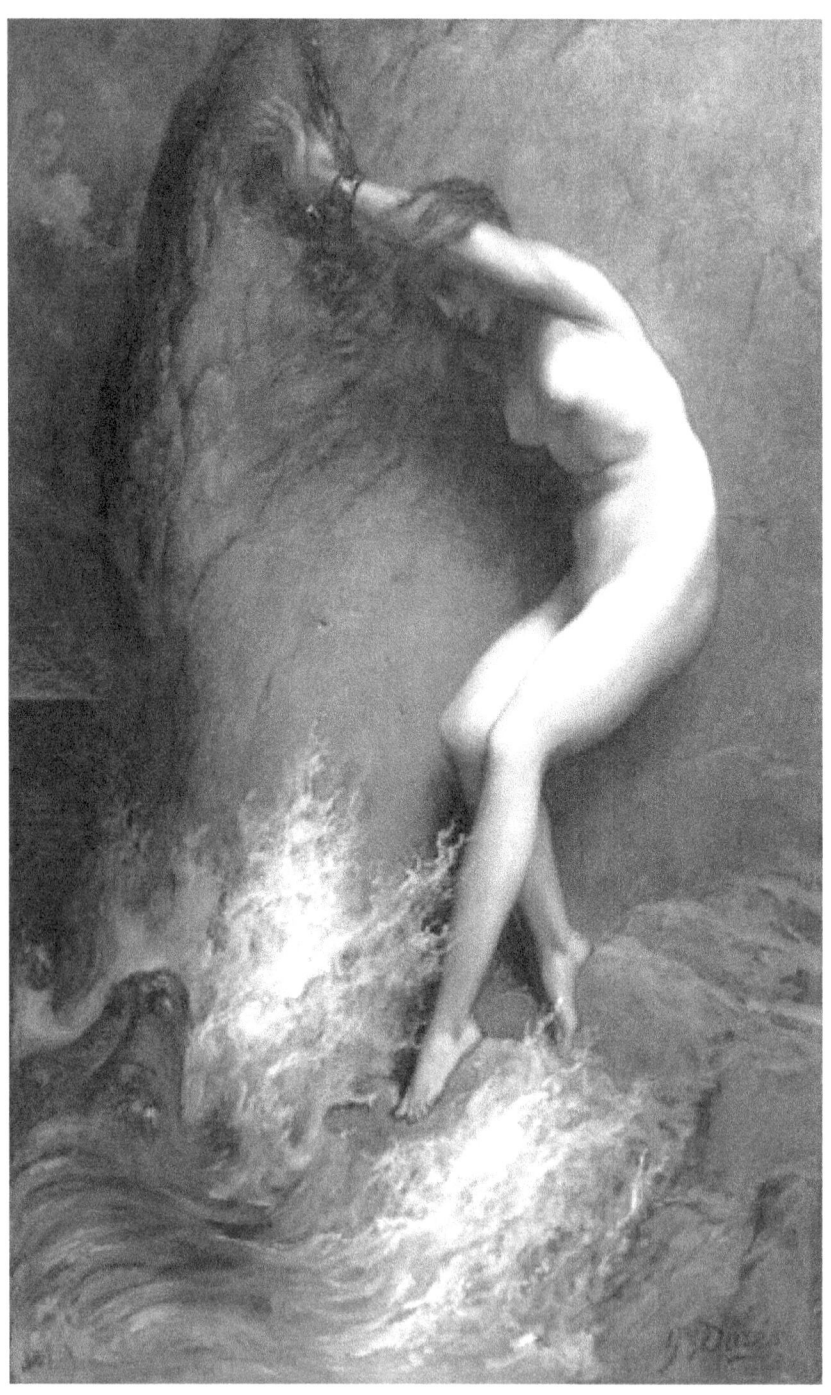

Gustave Doré

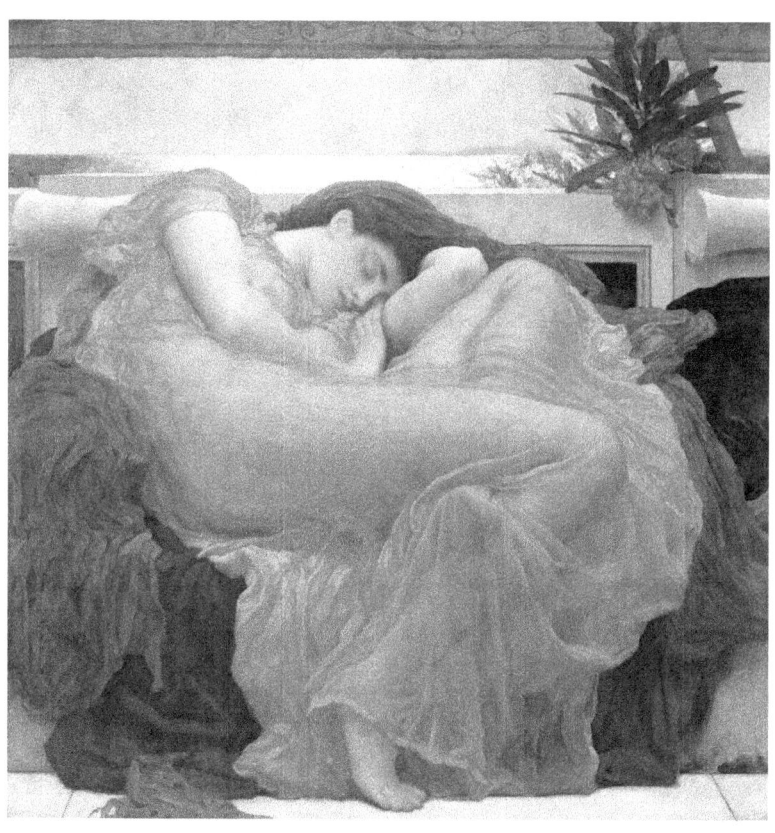

Lord Leighton, Flaming June, 1895, Puerto Rico

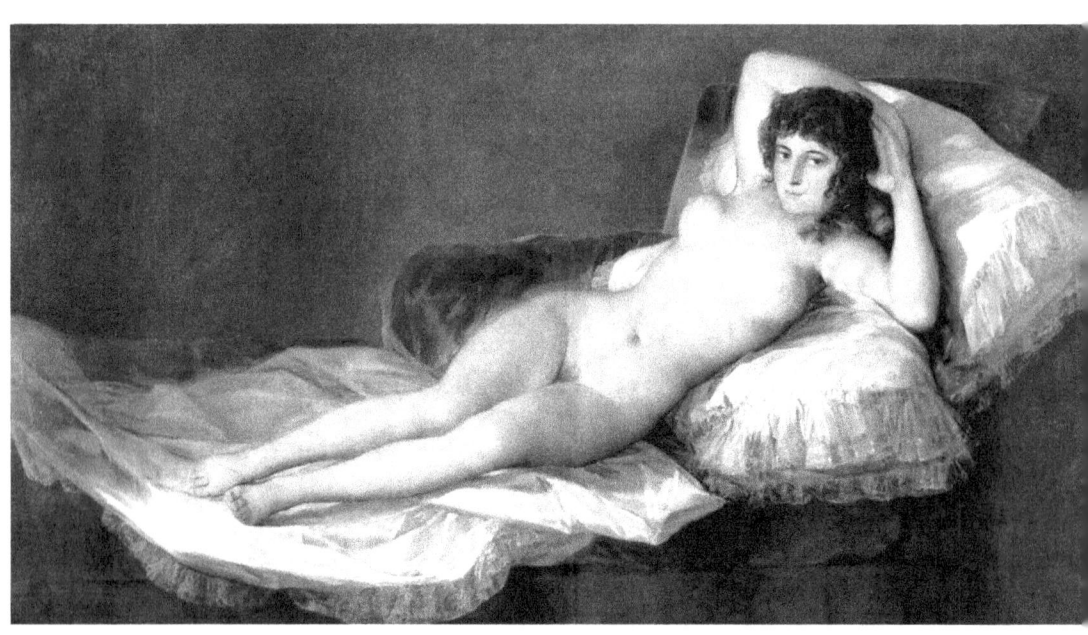

Francisco de Goya, Naked Maja, c. 1801, Prado, Madrid

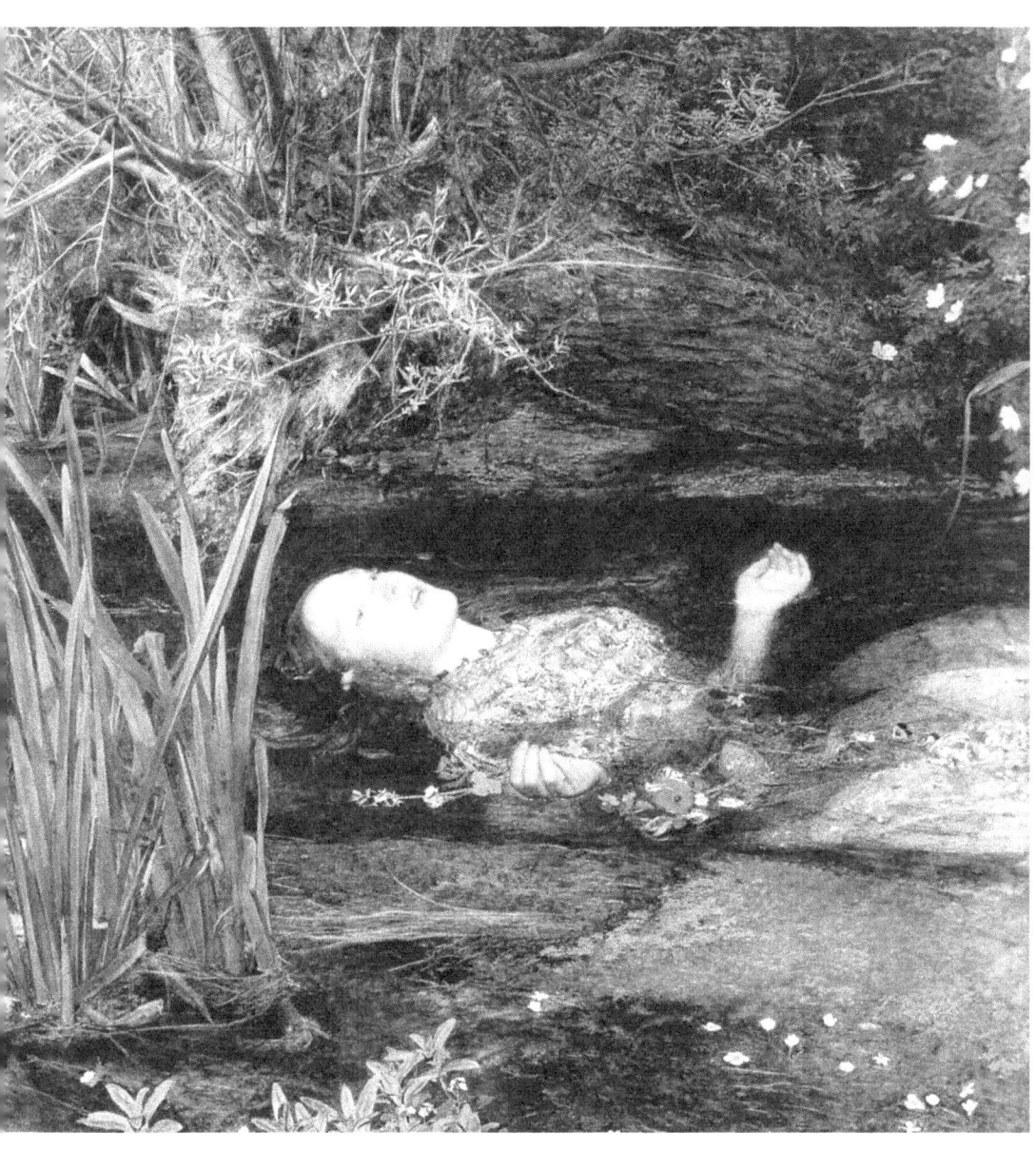

John Everett Millais, Ophelia.

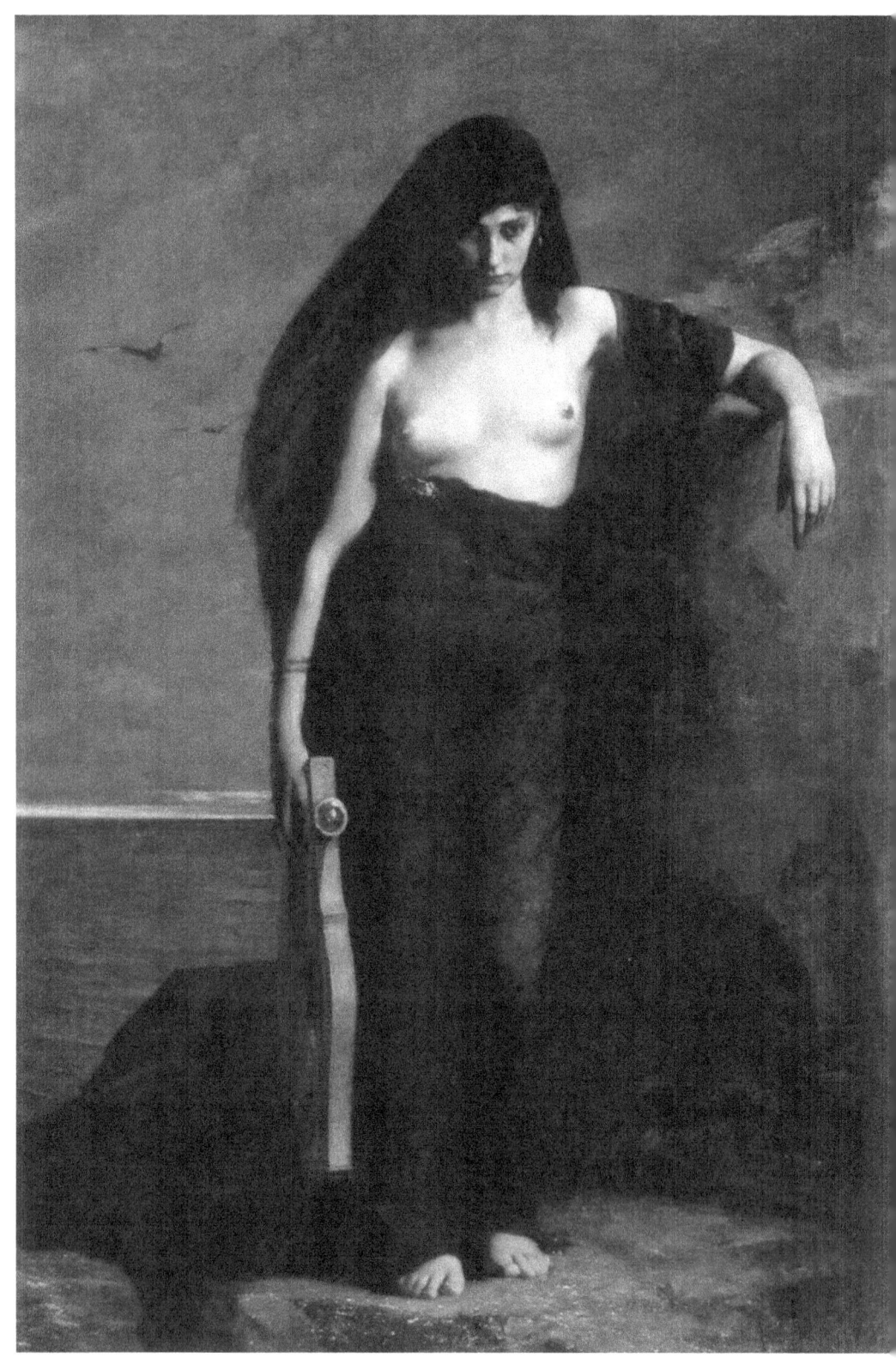

Charles Mengin, Sappho, 1867, Manchester

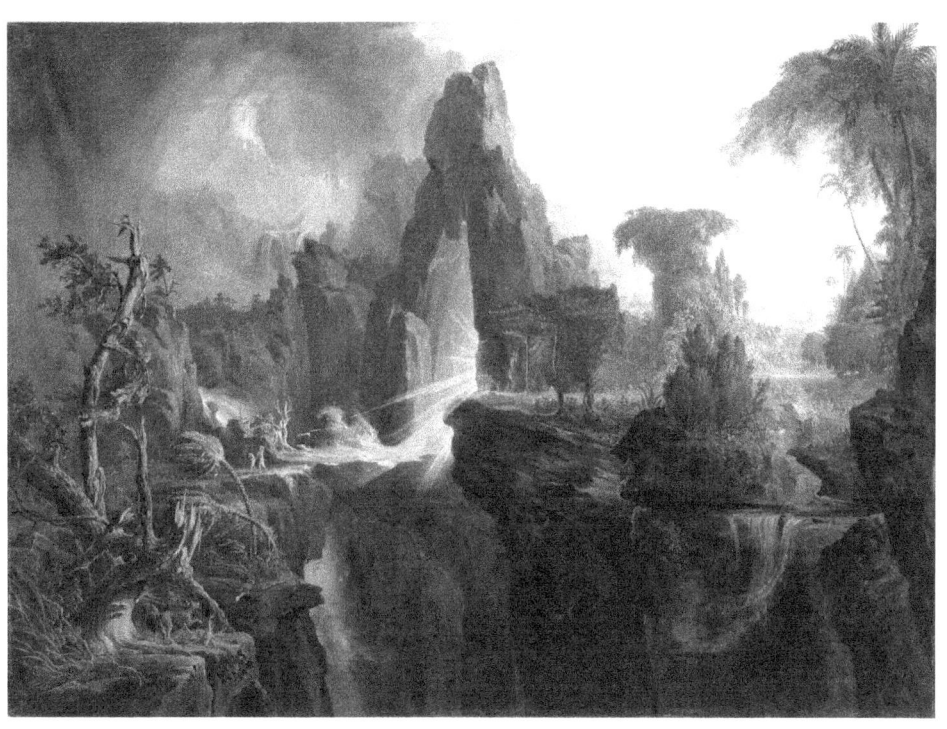

Thomas Cole, Expulsion From the Garden of Eden, 1828,
Museum of Fine Arts, Boston

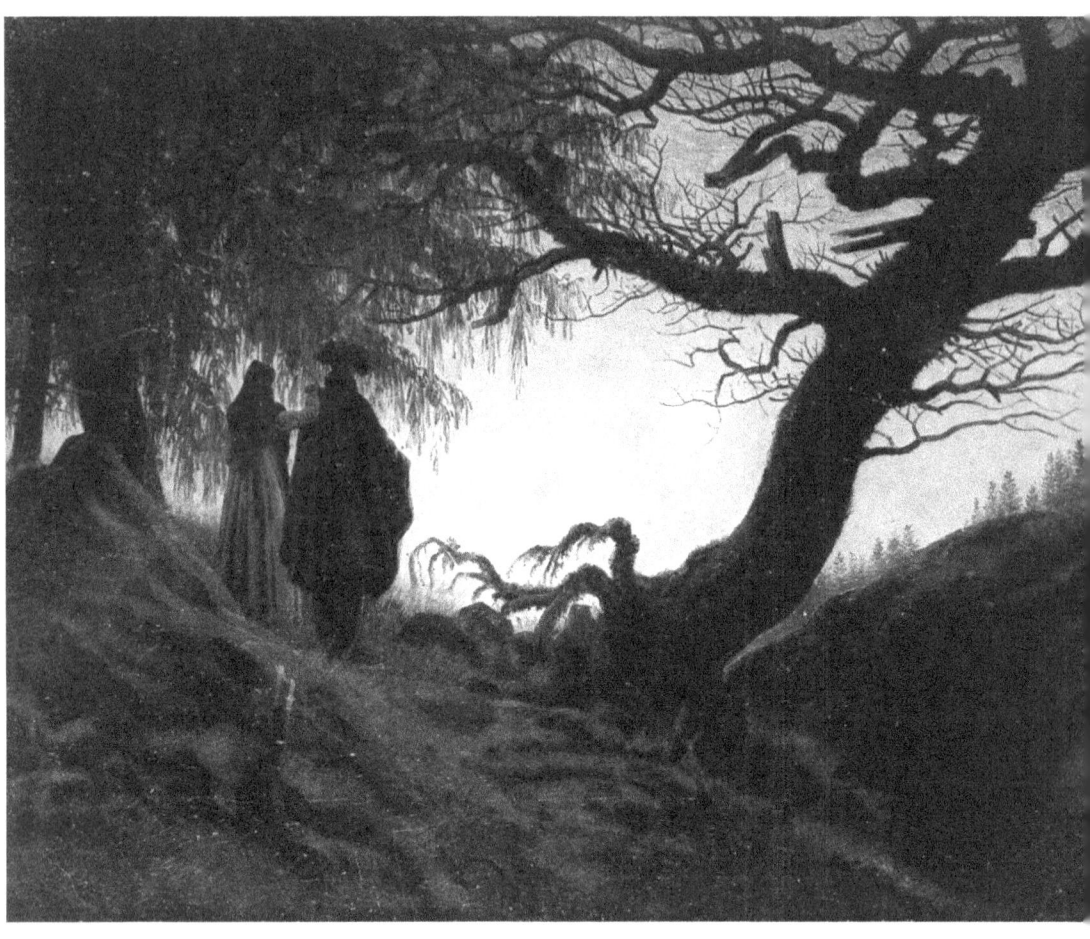

Caspar David Friedrich, Man and
Woman Contemplating the Moon,
1830-35, Alte Nationalgalerie

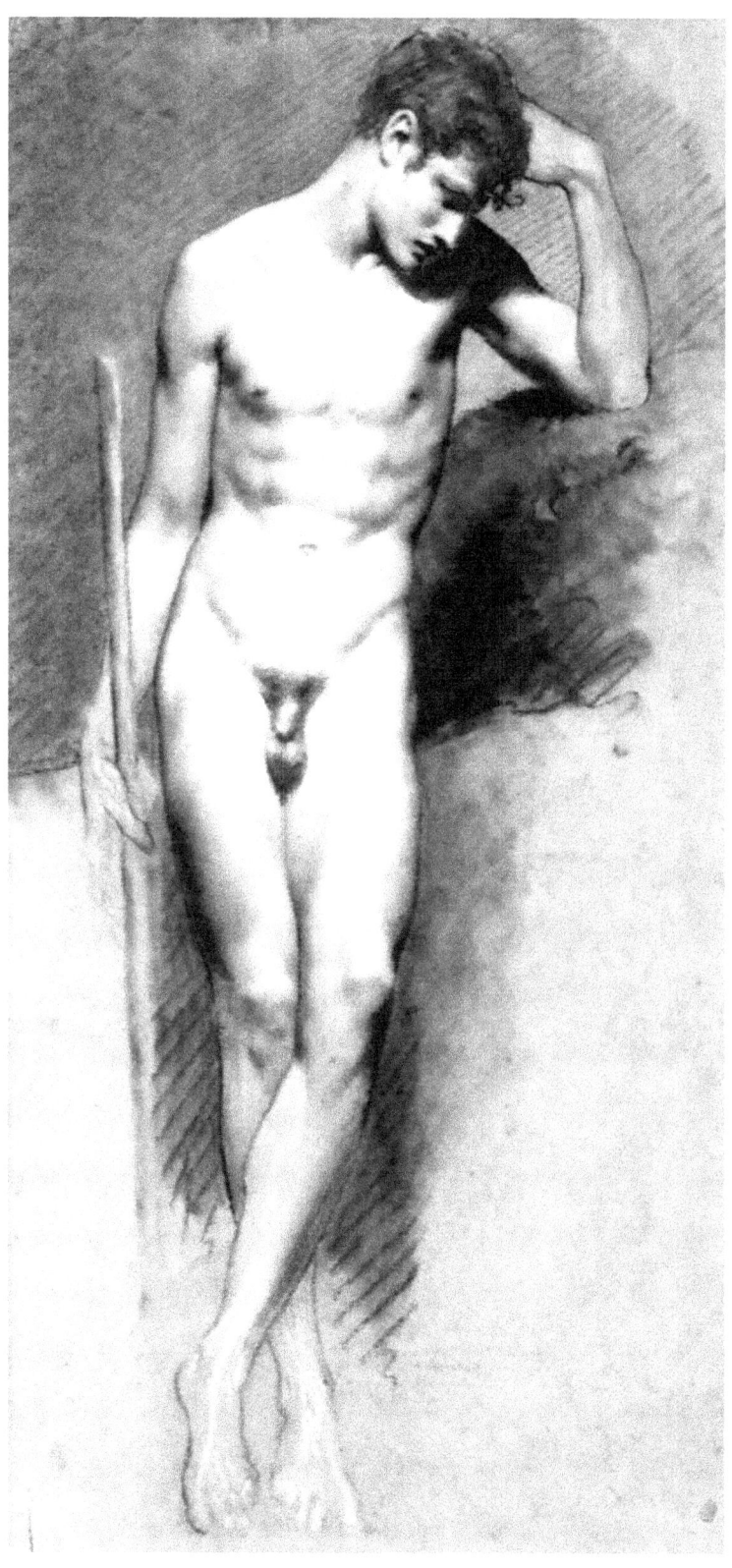

Pierre-Paul Prud'hon (1758-1823), Male Nude Standing

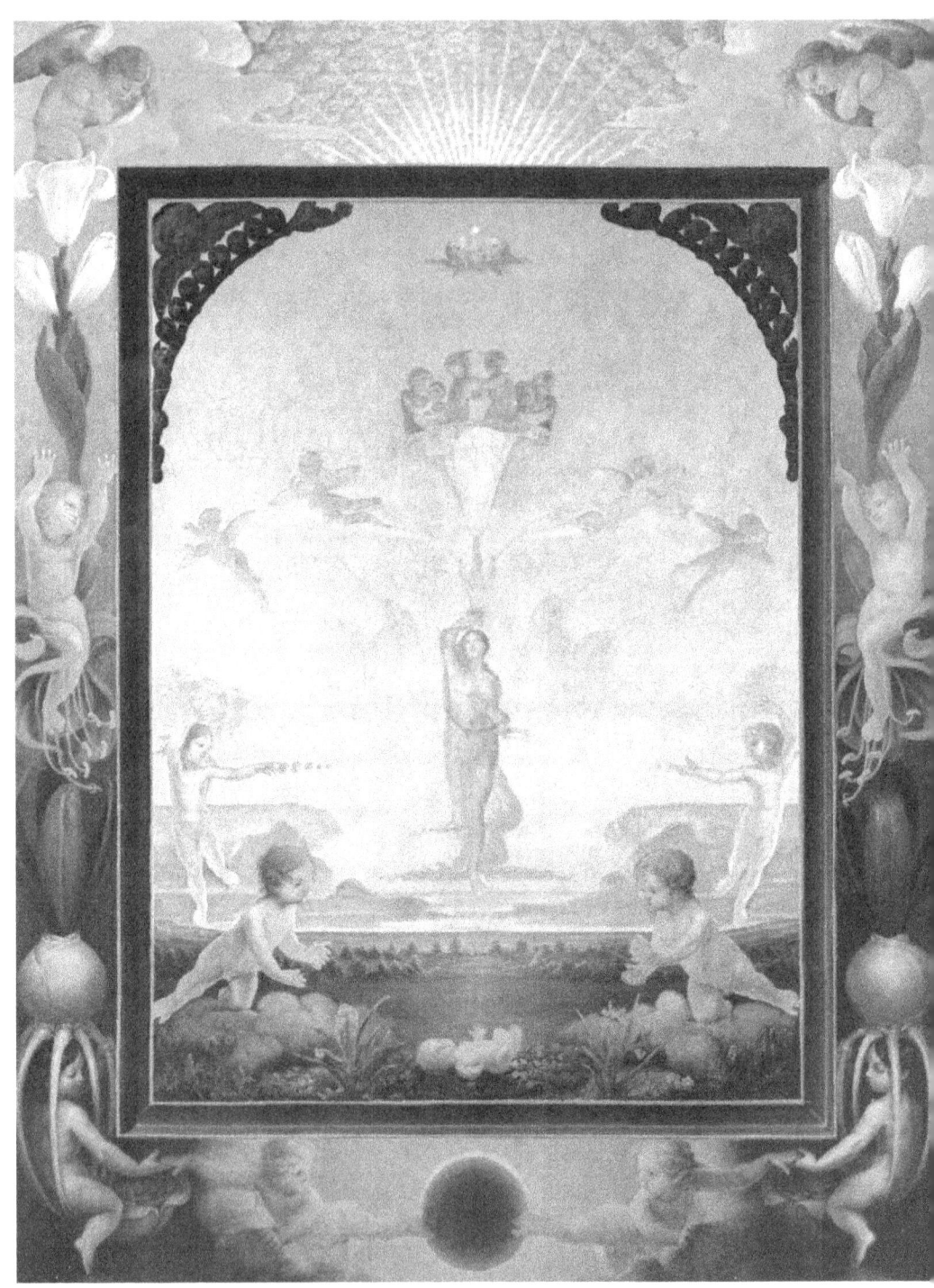

Philipp Otto Runge, Morning, 1808, Hamburg

J.M.W. Turner, The Blue Rigi, Lake of Lucerne, Sunrise,
1842, Clore Gallery, London

MAURICE SENDAK

& the art of children's book illustration

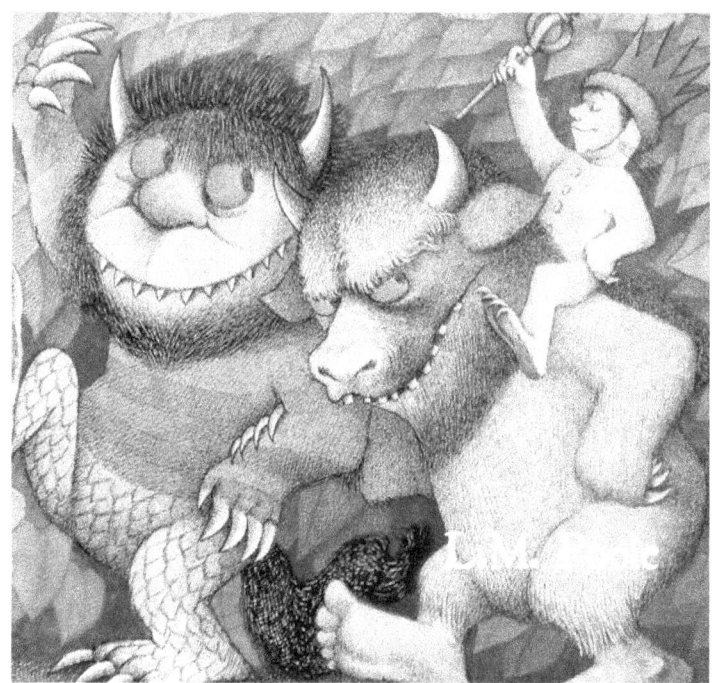

Maurice Sendak is the widely acclaimed American children's book author and illustrator. This critical study focuses on his famous trilogy, *Where the Wild Things Are*, *In the Night Kitchen* and *Outside Over There*, as well as the early works and Sendak's superb depictions of the Grimm Brothers' fairy tales in *The Juniper Tree*. L.M. Poole begins with a chapter on children's book illustration, in particular the treatment of fairy tales. Sendak's work is situated within the history of children's book illustration, and he is compared with many contemporary authors.

Fully illustrated. The book has been revised and updated for this edition.
ISBN 9781861714282 Pbk   ISBN 9781861713469 Hbk

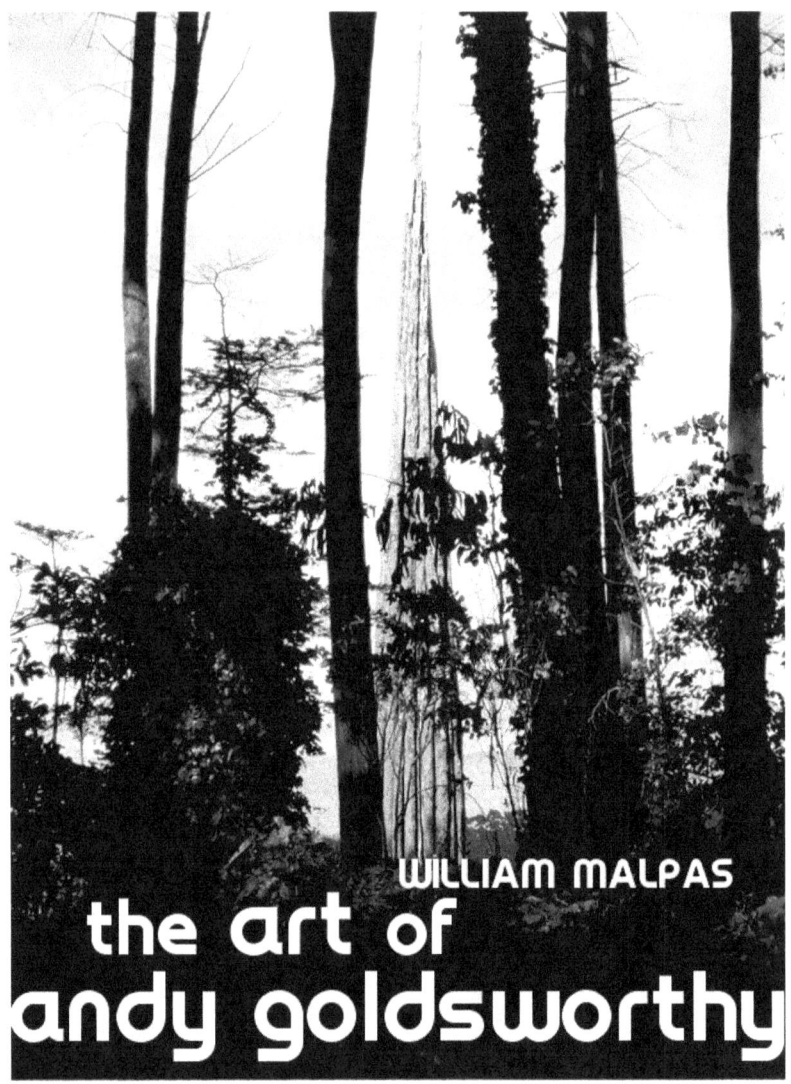

WILLIAM MALPAS
the art of
andy goldsworthy

This is the most comprehensive and detailed account of the art of Andy Goldsworthy available.

This study of Andy Goldsworthy discusses all of Goldsworthy's major exhibitions, books and projects, including the *Sheepfolds* project; *Garden of Stones* in New York; TV and dance collaborations; and the books *Wood, Stone, Time* and *Passage*. William Malpas surveys all of Goldsworthy's output, and analyzes his relation with other land artists such as Robert Smithson, the Christos, Walter de Maria, Chris Drury, Richard Long and David Nash; women sculptors; sculpture in the modern era; and Goldsworthy's place in the contemporary British art scene.

The book has been updated and revised for this new edition.

ISBN 9781861714107 Pbk   ISBN 9781861714114 Hbk
Fully illustrated   www.crmoon.com

Beauties, Beasts, and Enchantment

CLASSIC FRENCH FAIRY TALES

Translated and with an Introduction
by Jack Zipes

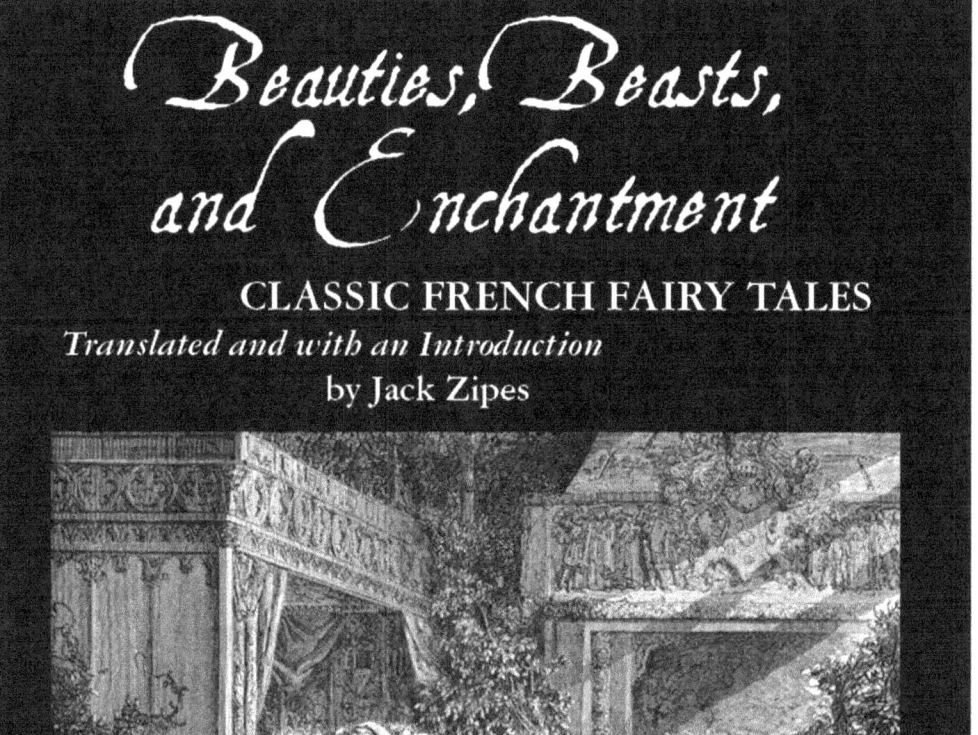

A collection of 36 classic French fairy tales translated by renowned writer Jack Zipes. *Cinderella*, *Beauty and the Beast*, *Sleeping Beauty* and *Little Red Riding Hood* are among the classic fairy tales in this amazing book.
Includes illustrations from fairy tale collections.
Jack Zipes has written and published widely on fairy tales.

'Terrific... a succulent array of 17th and 18th century 'salon' fairy tales'
- *The New York Times Book Review*

'These tales are adventurous, thrilling in a way fairy tales are meant to be... The translation from the French is modern, happily free of archaic and hyperbolic language... a fine and sophisticated collection' - *New York Tribune*

'Enjoyable to read... a unique collection of French regional folklore' - *Library Journal*

'Charming stories accompanied by attractive pen-and-ink drawings' - *Chattanooga Times*

Introduction and illustrations   612pp.   ISBN 9781861712510 Pbk   ISBN 9781861713193 Hbk

CRESCENT MOON PUBLISHING

web: www.crmoon.com e-mail: cresmopub@yahoo.co.uk

ARTS, PAINTING, SCULPTURE

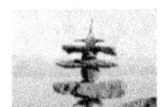
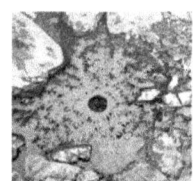
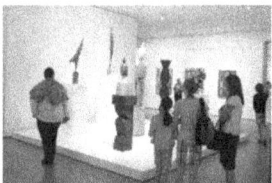

The Art of Andy Goldsworthy
Andy Goldsworthy: Touching Nature
Andy Goldsworthy in Close-Up
Andy Goldsworthy: Pocket Guide
Andy Goldsworthy In America
Land Art: A Complete Guide
The Art of Richard Long
Richard Long: Pocket Guide
Land Art In the UK
Land Art in Close-Up
Land Art In the U.S.A.
Land Art: Pocket Guide
Installation Art in Close-Up
Minimal Art and Artists In the 1960s and After
Colourfield Painting
Land Art DVD, TV documentary
Andy Goldsworthy DVD, TV documentary
The Erotic Object: Sexuality in Sculpture From Prehistory to the Present Day
Sex in Art: Pornography and Pleasure in Painting and Sculpture
Postwar Art
Sacred Gardens: The Garden in Myth, Religion and Art
Glorification: Religious Abstraction in Renaissance and 20th Century Art
Early Netherlandish Painting
Leonardo da Vinci
Piero della Francesca
Giovanni Bellini
Fra Angelico: Art and Religion in the Renaissance
Mark Rothko: The Art of Transcendence
Frank Stella: American Abstract Artist
Jasper Johns
Brice Marden
Alison Wilding: The Embrace of Sculpture
Vincent van Gogh: Visionary Landscapes
Eric Gill: Nuptials of God
Constantin Brancusi: Sculpting the Essence of Things
Max Beckmann
Caravaggio
Gustave Moreau
Egon Schiele: Sex and Death In Purple Stockings
Delizioso Fotografico Fervore: Works In Process 1
Sacro Cuore: Works In Process 2
The Light Eternal: J.M.W. Turner
The Madonna Glorified: Karen Arthurs

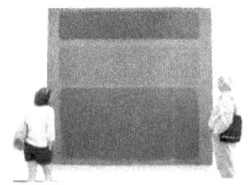
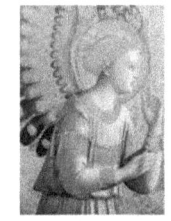
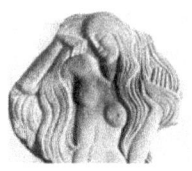
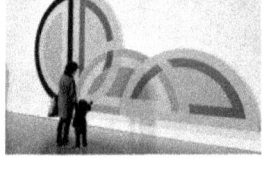
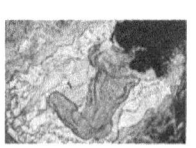
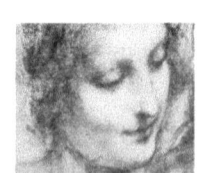
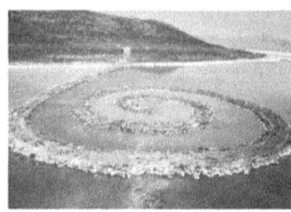

LITERATURE

J.R.R. Tolkien: The Books, The Films, The Whole Cultural Phenomenon
J.R.R. Tolkien: Pocket Guide
Tolkien's Heroic Quest
The *Earthsea* Books of Ursula Le Guin
Beauties, Beasts and Enchantment: Classic French Fairy Tales
German Popular Stories by the Brothers Grimm
Philip Pullman and *His Dark Materials*
Sexing Hardy: Thomas Hardy and Feminism
Thomas Hardy's *Tess of the d'Urbervilles*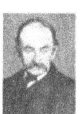
Thomas Hardy's *Jude the Obscure*
Thomas Hardy: The Tragic Novels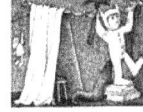
Love and Tragedy: Thomas Hardy
The Poetry of Landscape in Hardy
Wessex Revisited: Thomas Hardy and John Cowper Powys
Wolfgang Iser: Essays and Interviews
Petrarch, Dante and the Troubadours
Maurice Sendak and the Art of Children's Book Illustration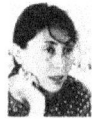
Andrea Dworkin
Cixous, Irigaray, Kristeva: The *Jouissance* of French Feminism
Julia Kristeva: Art, Love, Melancholy, Philosophy, Semiotics and Psychoanalysis
Hélène Cixous I Love You: The *Jouissance* of Writing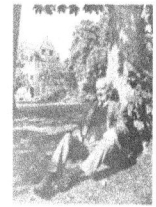
Luce Irigaray: Lips, Kissing, and the Politics of Sexual Difference
Peter Redgrove: Here Comes the Flood
Peter Redgrove: Sex-Magic-Poetry-Cornwall
Lawrence Durrell: Between Love and Death, East and West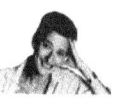
Love, Culture & Poetry: Lawrence Durrell
Cavafy: Anatomy of a Soul
German Romantic Poetry: Goethe, Novalis, Heine, Hölderlin
Feminism and Shakespeare
Shakespeare: Love, Poetry & Magic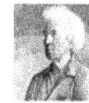
The Passion of D.H. Lawrence
D.H. Lawrence: Symbolic Landscapes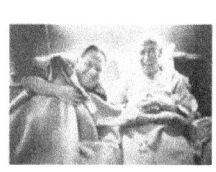
D.H. Lawrence: Infinite Sensual Violence
Rimbaud: Arthur Rimbaud and the Magic of Poetry
The Ecstasies of John Cowper Powys
Sensualism and Mythology: The Wessex Novels of John Cowper Powys
Amorous Life: John Cowper Powys and the Manifestation of Affectivity (H.W. Fawkner)
Postmodern Powys: New Essays on John Cowper Powys (Joe Boulter)
Rethinking Powys: Critical Essays on John Cowper Powys
Paul Bowles & Bernardo Bertolucci
Rainer Maria Rilke
Joseph Conrad: *Heart of Darkness*
In the Dim Void: Samuel Beckett
Samuel Beckett Goes into the Silence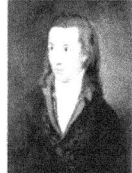
André Gide: Fiction and Fervour
Jackie Collins and the Blockbuster Novel
Blinded By Her Light: The Love-Poetry of Robert Graves
The Passion of Colours: Travels In Mediterranean Lands
Poetic Forms

POETRY

Ursula Le Guin: Walking In Cornwall
Peter Redgrove: Here Comes The Flood
Peter Redgrove: Sex-Magic-Poetry-Cornwall
Dante: Selections From the Vita Nuova
Petrarch, Dante and the Troubadours
William Shakespeare: Sonnets
William Shakespeare: Complete Poems
Blinded By Her Light: The Love-Poetry of Robert Graves
Emily Dickinson: Selected Poems
Emily Brontë: Poems
Thomas Hardy: Selected Poems
Percy Bysshe Shelley: Poems
John Keats: Selected Poems
Joh n Keats: Poems of 1820
D.H. Lawrence: Selected Poems
Edmund Spenser: Poems
Edmund Spenser: Amoretti
John Donne: Poems
Henry Vaughan: Poems
Sir Thomas Wyatt: Poems
Robert Herrick: Selected Poems
Rilke: Space, Essence and Angels in the Poetry of Rainer Maria Rilke
Rainer Maria Rilke: Selected Poems
Friedrich Hölderlin: Selected Poems
Arseny Tarkovsky: Selected Poems
Arthur Rimbaud: Selected Poems
Arthur Rimbaud: A Season in Hell
Arthur Rimbaud and the Magic of Poetry
Novalis: Hymns To the Night
German Romantic Poetry
Paul Verlaine: Selected Poems
Elizaethan Sonnet Cycles
D.J. Enright: By-Blows
Jeremy Reed: Brigitte's Blue Heart
Jeremy Reed: Claudia Schiffer's Red Shoes
Gorgeous Little Orpheus
Radiance: New Poems
Crescent Moon Book of Nature Poetry
Crescent Moon Book of Love Poetry
Crescent Moon Book of Mystical Poetry
Crescent Moon Book of Elizabethan Love Poetry
Crescent Moon Book of Metaphysical Poetry
Crescent Moon Book of Romantic Poetry
Pagan America: New American Poetry

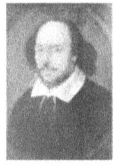
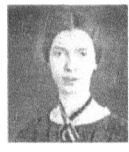

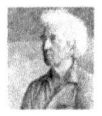
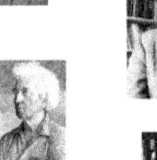
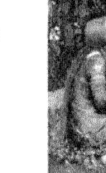
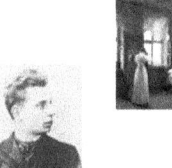
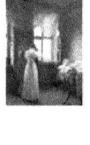
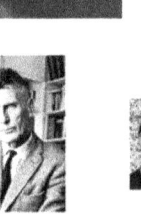
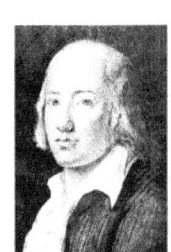
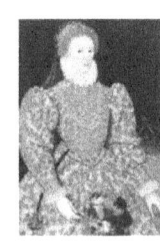

MEDIA, CINEMA, FEMINISM and CULTURAL STUDIES

J.R.R. Tolkien: The Books, The Films, The Whole Cultural Phenomenon
J.R.R. Tolkien: Pocket Guide
The *Lord of the Rings* Movies: Pocket Guide
The Cinema of Hayao Miyazaki
Hayao Miyazaki: *Princess Mononoke*: Pocket Movie Guide
Hayao Miyazaki: *Spirited Away*: Pocket Movie Guide
Tim Burton : Hallowe'en For Hollywood
Ken Russell
Ken Russell: *Tommy*: Pocket Movie Guide
The Ghost Dance: The Origins of Religion
The Peyote Cult
Cixous, Irigaray, Kristeva: The *Jouissance* of French Feminism
Julia Kristeva: Art, Love, Melancholy, Philosophy, Semiotics and Psychoanalysis
Luce Irigaray: Lips, Kissing, and the Politics of Sexual Difference
Hélene Cixous I Love You: The *Jouissance* of Writing
Andrea Dworkin
'Cosmo Woman': The World of Women's Magazines
Women in Pop Music
HomeGround: The Kate Bush Anthology
Discovering the Goddess (Geoffrey Ashe)
The Poetry of Cinema
The Sacred Cinema of Andrei Tarkovsky
Andrei Tarkovsky: Pocket Guide
Andrei Tarkovsky: *Mirror*: Pocket Movie Guide
Andrei Tarkovsky: *The Sacrifice*: Pocket Movie Guide
Walerian Borowczyk: Cinema of Erotic Dreams
Jean-Luc Godard: The Passion of Cinema
Jean-Luc Godard: *Hail Mary*: Pocket Movie Guide
Jean-Luc Godard: *Contempt*: Pocket Movie Guide
Jean-Luc Godard: *Pierrot le Fou*: Pocket Movie Guide
John Hughes and Eighties Cinema
Ferris Bueller's Day Off: Pocket Movie Guide
Jean-Luc Godard: Pocket Guide
The Cinema of Richard Linklater
Liv Tyler: Star In Ascendance
Blade Runner and the Films of Philip K. Dick
Paul Bowles and Bernardo Bertolucci
Media Hell: Radio, TV and the Press
An Open Letter to the BBC
Detonation Britain: Nuclear War in the UK
Feminism and Shakespeare
Wild Zones: Pornography, Art and Feminism
Sex in Art: Pornography and Pleasure in Painting and Sculpture
Sexing Hardy: Thomas Hardy and Feminism

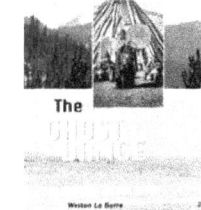
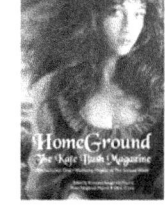
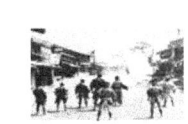
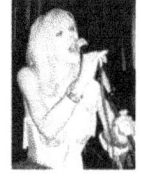
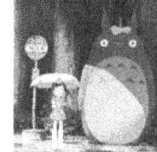

The Light Eternal is a model monograph, an exemplary job. The subject matter of the book is beautifully
organised and dead on beam. (Lawrence Durrell)
It is amazing for me to see my work treated with such passion and respect. (Andrea Dworkin)

CRESCENT MOON PUBLISHING
P.O. Box 1312, Maidstone, Kent, ME14 5XU, Great Britain. www.crmoon.com

cresmopub@yahoo.co.uk   www.crescentmoon.org.uk

www.ingramcontent.com/pod-product-compliance
Lightning Source LLC
Chambersburg PA
CBHW051327220526
45468CB00004B/1536